A QUEST FOR FULFILMENT

JAMES ORPWOOD

With a Foreword by Roger Bayzand

Grosvenor House
Publishing Limited

The right of James Orpwood to be identified as the author of this
work has been asserted in accordance with Section 78
of the Copyright, Designs and Patents Act 1988.

The book cover is copyright to James Orpwood

This book is published by
Grosvenor House Publishing Ltd
Link House
140 The Broadway, Tolworth, Surrey, KT6 7HT.
www.grosvenorhousepublishing.co.uk

A CIP record for this book
is available from the British Library

ISBN 978-1-83975-243-8

Every effort has been made to obtain the necessary permissions with
reference to copyrighted material. We apologise for any omissions in this
respect and will be pleased to make the appropriate acknowledgements in
future editions. Photos remain the copyright of the original photographer;
are credited as such and included gratefully with permission.

A Quest For Fulfilment is a work of non-fiction. Every effort has been made to
obtain the necessary permissions with reference to people named in the
book.

Cover designed by James Orpwood. **Main picture:** On the summit of Bynack More,
Cairngorms. Photo by the author. **Inset:** The author. © Wendell Martin, 2017.

In fond memory of

Richard "Dick" Baker
and
Peter "Tibby" Tybinkowski.

"Not all the young want to run away. Far from it. Some of them love these wild places with devotion and ask nothing better than to spend their lives in them."

Nan Shepherd, *The Living Mountain*

Contents

Foreword

When I first met James he was 14 and being delivered to my charter fishing boat by his somewhat apprehensive-looking parents. Launching into the rough and tumble of a day at sea with a bunch of much older anglers might be daunting to some but young James took it in his stride. In fact although he was quiet he was obviously listening and picked up the fishing techniques straight away. He became a regular on the trips and was obviously a keen and dedicated angler who became very proficient, to the extent that I could use him as an example when someone was struggling, hence the saying "Watch James, he is rather good at this!"

It was no surprise to me when, after a successful university education, he entered fishery science and I quite expected him to end up as head of a research station, or perhaps a university professor. Therefore to hear he had changed tack and become a mountain leader was intriguing and something I would like to hear more about.

Thank you for writing this entertaining book, James. Now I understand the change as you, very much like me, found a love of taking people to do and see things that will live with them for ever.

Best wishes to you and Ellen; keep creating memories.

Roger Bayzand
Retired top charter fishing boat skipper
Award-winning artist

Prologue

I was alone, sat on a huge rock, resting my weary legs and gazing at the mountains. I had adopted a similar position many times, only the rocks and the mountains changed. A short distance in front of me, I could see the top of the steep slope leading to the valley far below. A few hours previously I had walked up that slope, glad when it had finally abated and I had caught my first glimpse of the beautiful little lake, now behind me. It had reminded me a little of walking up the slope from the Hutchison Memorial Hut to Loch Etchachan in the Cairngorms, the way the slope eases abruptly and the loch suddenly appears in front of you. But I wasn't in the Cairngorms, or even in Scotland. I was in the Himalayas. Lobuche East Base Camp to be precise, at an altitude of over 5,000 m.

It was a stunning spot, nestling in a small hollow with the slopes of our objective, Lobuche East (6,119 m), towering above. In front of me, the afternoon clouds had filled in the valleys at my feet. Yet at this altitude, I was above the clouds, in the midst of some of the highest mountains in the world. The sun was slinking down behind me and, as darkness claimed the valleys below, the last of the day's sunlight illuminated the peaks of Ama Dablam and Taweche. The white peaks turned orange, then pink, before darkness swallowed the scene.

I swung my feet idly. It had been a strenuous day of trekking, starting from Dzonglha that morning and, lovely as the group was, I was glad to have some time to myself. I had never really thought of myself as a "people person", but a shared love of the mountains seemed to be changing that.

Any last remnants of the day's warmth had disappeared with the sun and it was very cold. I retreated, metaphorically at least, a little further into my cosy down jacket which did little to flatter my "rucksack-on-legs" figure. Before switching on my headlamp and making my way back to the tent, I looked up into the black sky. It was full of stars, thousands of them. Immediately, my eyes were drawn to a distinctive shape in the night sky - three particularly recognisable stars, more or less evenly spaced in a straight line - which my father and I refer to as "my three stars", more commonly known as Orion's Belt. I was astonished. The same three stars I had gazed up at whilst night fishing on a beach on the south coast of England many years ago were visible here, many thousands of miles away. They had a timeless beauty, connecting my past with the present.

But what about my future? My love of fish and fishing had taken me, quite naturally, into a scientific career, yet back home in Scotland, and here in the Himalayas, it was my love of the mountains which was inspiring me now, fulfilling me in a way I never could have imagined. Would I be a fool to try and turn my hobby and passion into my career once again?

I wandered back to the tent. Out here, in the mountains, I was as happy as I had ever been. It wasn't only the rocks and the mountains which had changed. I had changed too.

Chapter 1

Early Years

A few years ago, I had the pleasure of introducing my niece, Millie, and nephew, Ted, to the delights of tiddler fishing in a New Forest stream. Old habits die hard and, paddling around bare-footed with a hand net, it was fabulous to rekindle my childhood memories from family holidays. With an impressive haul of bullheads and minnows up to a respectable inch-and-a-half in length occupying the large clear plastic jar, Millie noted perceptively, "You're quite good at this, James!" Had she not been so young, I would have shared with her the first phrase that came to mind - from *Only Fools and Horses* when, losing to Del Boy during a game of cards, Boycie utters, "I've had plenty of bloody practice!"

Millie could not have known the irony of her wonderfully insightful comment, but she was right. I was good at catching fish and I'd had lots of practice. I had spent most of my childhood paddling in streams and grubbing around on the sea shore, before going on to acquire over a decade of angling experience, rubbing shoulders with some of the best in the business. This love of fish and fishing had led me, quite naturally, to study and then work with fish for many years. So where did mountains fit into this? Why was this "grown-up" tiddler catcher working so hard to pursue a very different career path, retraining so he could share his love of Scotland's mountains and wild places with others? More to the point, where did *"quite* good" come into it?!

* * * * * *

As a child I lived in Iver, a village in Buckinghamshire, England, just outside West London and close to Slough, Windsor and Heathrow Airport. Back in the day, my parents recall a traditional small village amid pleasant countryside and farmland, far removed from the modern urban sprawl of that area today.

I am one of three children, with two older sisters, Fiona (the eldest) and Kate. My father worked as a telephone engineer, whilst my mother had stopped paid work when children began to arrive on the scene, returning to part-time work as an administrative assistant in a local school when my sisters and I were old enough to make our own way to school and suchlike. Blessed to be raised in a loving home, as youngsters my sisters and I enjoyed watching the local farmers working in the fields behind our house, riding our bikes around the quiet lanes and countryside and building dens in the woods.

We were a close-knit family and, although my sisters and I had the usual sibling squabbles, if anyone outside of the family dared to pick on any one of us, the other two children would quickly leap to their defence. One memorable recollection of Kate's protectiveness towards me occurred whilst playing by a river one day. By all accounts (I was too young to remember), I had built a sand castle and very proud I was too. A child from another family came over to see what I was up to. He had no clothes on whatsoever, enjoying the uninhibited freedom which comes with being a young child, and proceeded to pee on my sand castle! This was greeted with horror by Kate, who apparently did no more than turn around and hit the child! It was no doubt left to my parents to practise a little diplomacy and explain to his parents what had happened. Or perhaps we all just ran away. I don't remember.

Fish, mountains, and getting wet; three things which have dominated my life so far, featured from my earliest days. During a visit to a trout farm whilst on holiday in the Cotswolds, I discovered to my cost that my little red Wellington boots offered somewhat less grip than might ideally be required, at least to a small boy stood on a wet, sloping grass bank next to a pool of water. Leaning over enthusiastically to feed the fish, I was happily throwing my trout pellets with gay abandon. So keen was I to get a closer look, the next thing I knew (and it's the only part of the day I remember), I was in the water taking some early swimming lessons. Even then, fish proved how difficult they could be to catch, with not a single trout finding its way into my jacket, much to my father's disappointment. A fresh trout for tea might have gone some way to make up for his soaking - it was he who picked the short straw, jumping in to fish me out.

Mountains featured for the first time during two holidays the family enjoyed in the Lake District. The first of these was quite an adventure, setting off on the train from Watford Junction with all our stuff for two weeks contained in nine small rucksacks. Getting off the train at Oxenholme, it was then just a short train ride to Windermere and our accommodation. We climbed the Old Man of Coniston and explored lots of other lovely places on that holiday and hoped to return soon.

A year later, it was the day before returning to the Lake District for another holiday. Kate and I had been sent off to the cinema in Slough to get us out from under our parents' feet so they could pack the nine rucksacks once again. It was 1991 and we saw, for the first time, the hit film *Robin Hood: Prince of Thieves*, a film we saw many times subsequently and still one of my favourites. Rucksacks packed, we were dab hands at the whole train thing by now, and back to Windermere we went. We were definitely more adventurous on this holiday, climbing Helvellyn from Wythburn, which, at the time, seemed like quite a big day. Being fair, I think it *is* quite a big day, but especially at the age of only 10!

However, a few days later, the climb of Helvellyn was eclipsed by an absolute epic. Catching an early bus from Windermere to Keswick, we walked to Watendlath via Ashness Bridge, a famous stone-built bridge, the picture of which adorns many a box of Lakeland fudge. So far so good. We continued the walk by heading up across the fells from Watendlath, but got what I have come to know as "temporarily cartographically challenged", or, to put it another way, lost. Thankfully, after some rest, a little assistance from some passers-by and helped by the fact that we recognised the distinctive shape of Helvellyn on the opposite side of the Thirlmere valley, we were soon back in business. We eventually located Blea Tarn before dropping to Harrop Tarn and Wythburn as planned. We caught the return bus to Windermere, the last of the day, with just minutes to spare. Despite being so young, this day proved something that has become so apparent since - it is the epics which are remembered most fondly! Outdoor instructors often talk about type I fun and type II fun, the former being when it's fun at the time, the latter being when it's fun back in the safety of the warm bar at the end of the day. That day was definitely type II fun, without the benefit of the bar.

Getting wet featured through it all. Back then - and I'm not that old - there was no "school run". We took the bus to school, rode our bikes, or walked. If it rained, we got wet and got on with it. Riding my bike did prove trickier on one occasion when, after school one day, I had been to a local hospital to have a couple of ingrown toe nails removed. That in itself was not the most pleasant experience in the world. However, with substantial bandages on my feet for several days after the operation, the only footwear I could wear was a slightly larger pair of Wellington boots than those which ended their days in the bottom of the trout farm. Riding home from hospital in those was about as easy as performing a ballet dance in a pair of lead boots, and no more gracious. Nonetheless, it served as good practice for later times, when I would wobble away on my bike to go bait digging on the sea shore. Off I would go, with Wellington boots on my feet (by then an even bigger pair), a fork strapped to the crossbar, and, swinging from the handlebars, a very large bucket which, I hoped, would soon be full of worms.

As the Sheriff of Nottingham, played by the peerless late Alan Rickman, said in that wonderful film, "It's amazing I'm sane!"

As children, our holidays were always the highlights of the year. As well as those occasional forays to the Cotswolds and the Lake District, it was Lymington and the New Forest where we went for most of our holidays as far back as I can remember. Here, we became something of experts at tiddler fishing, typically enjoying a walk or bike ride in the New Forest and having a picnic lunch by a stream, where we would paddle and catch any number of small fish with a hand net. We would keep the fish in a large clear plastic jar full of fresh water for just a few minutes - long enough to admire their striking colours and features - before returning them carefully to their home. We delighted in catching minnows, sticklebacks, stone loach and bullheads, and were particularly chuffed if we managed to net a small brown trout (incredibly quick) or eel (all-round slippery customers). We were also fascinated by the sea shore, turning over rocks before replacing them as we found them, often finding shore crabs, limpets, barnacles, anemones and small fish such as blennies and gobies. Lymington is a town with a regular ferry service to the Isle of Wight, and we would occasionally be treated to a day on the island. Freshwater Bay was a favourite spot and, taking our bikes over on the ferry, we could ride along an old railway track bed to get there from Yarmouth.

It became something of a tradition that, on the last afternoon of our holiday, after our picnic by a stream in the New Forest, we would make our way to the sea at Milford before returning to Lymington alongside the marshes and mudflats. The views out across the Solent, the strip of sea between the mainland and the Isle of Wight, were superb, and Hurst Castle seemed to dominate the view from many directions. This area was a true paradise for us children, freed from the shackles of school and blissfully unaware of the often harsh realities of adult life which would come later. On more than one occasion I can remember the three of us crying on our last evening, not wanting to go home.

Back home in Iver, I began to go fishing "properly", i.e. with rod and line (angling). This was helped by a friend in school who was keen, a couple of lads who lived on my street, and my father who used to fish as a young man. Iver was a great location for fishing, with several good rivers nearby, myriad gravel pits in the Colne Valley, several natural lakes, and the Grand Union Canal. I quickly picked up the basics and still recall my first-ever fish caught on rod and line - a small perch caught at Black Park Lake. Perch are very attractive, with bright red fins and green flanks overlaid with dark stripes. As with many fish, their colours are expressed more vividly when they live in clear water and, as Black Park Lake was crystal clear, so my first perch was a very pretty fish!

Fishing very soon became an obsession and we began exploring many of our local venues. I enjoyed learning the art of watercraft, "reading" the water and learning about why certain species of fish live in particular places, what food they might be looking for and therefore what bait might be used to tempt them. The number of species I caught grew rapidly. My first pike came as something of a welcome bonus, a feisty 3 lb. "jack", as small pike up to about 7 lb. in weight are known, that, surprisingly, took a single maggot during another trip to Black Park Lake. I also enjoyed my first taste of angling stardom around this time! Well, perhaps not quite, but I was very excited when a picture of me holding a beautiful 4 lb. tench appeared in the *Angling Times*. It was one of two tench I caught that day, the other weighing 3 lb., fishing at local Farlow's Lake.

My fishing moved up a notch when Fiona went to university. I took on her newspaper delivery round whilst she was away during term time and enjoyed the new-found freedom that £15 a week gave me. With my first week's wages I bought a big green fishing umbrella. I also joined a local angling club which had the fishing rights to a couple of stretches of my local rivers. The club would swap venues with other clubs for days out, so I could travel with some of our club members to fish elsewhere. The club had a very active match (competition) calendar and soon I was competing regularly on our beloved River Colne, as well as travelling to the Rivers Cherwell and Thame in Oxfordshire, the River Stour in Dorset, and various stretches of the Rivers Thames and Kennet in Berkshire, to name a few. These venues were a long way from Iver and, as a young lad of about 12 or 13 years old, I was very lucky that the club members generously gave me lifts to these far-flung places, all well beyond cycling distance! They were an extremely kindly bunch and I was very grateful for their encouragement. I learnt loads from these experiences and it was sad that in the end I was only in this angling club for about a year.

The family loved the New Forest and Lymington and, eventually, my parents took the plunge and decided to move there, something which had always been on the cards, but could now become a reality. Fiona was away at university, and Kate would follow suit in the coming autumn. My father had been made redundant from his telephone engineering job some years previously, and had worked tirelessly in a number of casual jobs to keep an income coming in. This was a great example to set and I learnt not to be too proud to turn your hand to anything to earn a few pounds. Having decided to move, my father secured a job as a site officer at an educational establishment near Lymington. He spent a period of time living away from home during the weeks whilst I stayed in Iver with my mother and Kate, the plan being that Kate would finish her A-levels before we moved, and I could finish the school year before starting my GSCEs in my new school in Hampshire. However, the family home in Iver sold more quickly than expected, meaning we needed somewhere to stay locally for a few months. Luckily, some friends of my parents heard of our predicament and offered us accommodation in nearby Colnbrook until the end of the school year, when my mother, Kate and I would move to meet up with my father down in Lymington.

In 1995, at the age of 14, I moved to Lymington, a childhood dream come true. During these early years, I had developed a deep appreciation for the natural world around me. This proved to have a profound effect on where I would head in life, although at this point I didn't realise just how much there was to know about fish hiding under stones! Nonetheless, I was very happy that a fish-filled future now seemed guaranteed.

Chapter 2

The Famous "Red-Hot Kettle"

Shortly before moving to Lymington I joined the Lymington and District Sea Fishing Club, a large and very active organisation with a strong junior section and a busy calendar of shore and boat angling competitions and other trips throughout the year. I already knew that Lymington was an excellent place to be based if you love fishing. The prospect of living near the sea definitely appealed to me and I readily turned my attention to sea fishing and another steep learning curve began.

On a weekend visit to Lymington from Colnbrook in May 1995, a couple of months before our move, I went on my first club boat trip on Sundance II, skippered by Roger Bayzand. Widely regarded as one of the top charter fishing boat skippers in Britain, Roger was a regular contributor to the angling press and I had often gazed in awe at photos of smiling anglers holding huge fish caught on Sundance II. To say I was excited would be an understatement!

That day was a wreck trip, and proved to be the first of many for me over the coming years. Wreck fishing does not involve fishing for wrecks (although wrecks are ridiculously easy to hook!) but fishing over some of the many wrecks lying in the English Channel between the Isle of Wight and France. These trips were typically 12 hours long, leaving the quayside at 7 a.m., steaming for perhaps three hours or so to reach the wrecks in mid Channel, fishing for several hours, before returning to port around 7 p.m. Heading 30 or more miles south of the Needles, the famous chalk stacks marking the extreme western end of the Isle of Wight, in a 34-foot boat, losing sight of land for many hours, was quite an adventure even without the fishing. The time spent steaming out to the wrecks always passed fairly quickly.

Anglers are a friendly bunch and, particularly on my first-ever wreck trip, they were keen to help this new lad who had just joined the club. There were magazines to peruse and a very impressive photo album full of pictures of beaming anglers displaying their fish caught aboard the boat. There was also the famous "red-hot kettle", Roger's seemingly ever-boiling kettle providing a continuous stream of hot tea and coffee, guaranteed to warm the cockles! Putting the world to rights, or at least attempting to, was always a feature of the long haul out to mid Channel, as well as sorting tackle and generally preparing for the day ahead. On that first trip I didn't have my own tackle, but watched with interest and listened as my hire kit was prepared for me. At that time, Sundance II was sponsored by tackle giant Shimano, and by the time we arrived at the wreck, I was proudly sporting a new Shimano hat which would accompany me on many fishing trips until it eventually rusted away a decade later.

This was a completely different style of fishing to anything I had done before, and was quite a step up for a 14-year-old lad who had only been coarse fishing for a couple of years. Pollock were the target species; hard-fighting, sight-feeding fish targeted with lures whilst drifting over the wreck. This was very exciting fishing as it was quite involved and required a lot of skill from the skipper and the anglers. Once the wreck had been located, the skipper would set the boat uptide of the wreck so that, when the engines were switched off, the boat would drift over the wreck, carried by the tide.

The fishing technique was to drop your lure to the bottom and then retrieve it, but not all the way to the top, counting as you went. Pollock could be located at different depths in the water column and part of the skill was to work out where they were on that day, and at different stages of the tide. A good rule of thumb was to wind up for 45 turns of the reel handle. If you didn't get a take you would drop the lure back to the bottom and retrieve it for 45 turns again. At some point, as the boat was about to pass directly over the wreck (as shown by the echo sounder), the skipper would shout "WRECK", the signal to wind in sufficiently so your fishing gear didn't snag the wreck as you drifted over it, which would result in lost tackle. Once the boat had drifted past the wreck the skipper would shout "CLEAR", indicating it was safe to drop your lure back to the bottom and start another retrieve. Tuned-in anglers would watch the echo sounder themselves and would often take a chance at dropping their gear just before clearing the wreck. This risked tackle losses but, if you had timed it just right, meant that when the shout "CLEAR" came, your lure would have hit the bottom and you would be starting to retrieve. This spot tucked right in behind the wreck was often a top place to pick up fish when the tide was running hard as they would be sheltering behind the wreck, rather like standing behind a wall when it's windy. Little did I realise at this time the extent to which I would come to understand fish sheltering behaviour! Once the boat was some distance downtide of the wreck, all the anglers would wind their gear up to the surface and the skipper would start the engines and drive the boat round ready for another drift.

When a fish took your lure it was very exciting and the adrenaline would always start pumping. Initially you would feel a series of plucks as the fish came up behind the lure and nipped at the end of it. The trick was not to "strike" but to keep winding so the fish would engulf the lure, turn, and dive for the bottom. The rod would bend over alarmingly and you would be forced to stop winding. The clutch on the reel would be set so the fish could take line without breaking it and, as the fish dived, all you could do was hold on tightly as the rod bent double and line poured off the reel. I can vividly remember my first pollock and, tipping the scales down to a healthy 11 ½ lb., it was the largest of four I caught that day. It was an incredible experience and I was well and truly "hooked".

Returning to the quayside early evening, I slept in the car all the way back to Colnbrook. Needless to say, school the following day was just a little duller than usual in comparison, albeit the day brightened up when my mother and I visited Boots after school to have my photos developed using their 1-hour processing service. This was before the days of digital cameras - just imagine having to wait for a whole day to see your photos! Eagerly awaiting their arrival, we enjoyed a drink in the café. The photos did not disappoint and, being quite a small lad, an 11 ½ lb. pollock looked pretty impressive when held up, with any lack of stature on my part being more than compensated for by the size of my grin. Roger appeared to share this sentiment and, unbeknown to us, kindly submitted a similar photo to the *Southern Daily Echo*. I was dead chuffed!

Over the next decade I was to enjoy many wonderful boat fishing trips. The club generally had one trip a month from March to December. Between March and May, these were wreck trips and we would target pollock. By the middle of this period, depending on the tides and the weather, the first of the cod would begin to show on the mid-Channel wrecks. These could be big, and I witnessed one which tipped the scales down to 32 lb. I never caught one that big, but did catch a few cod on the wrecks up to 14 lb. Drift fishing with lures using relatively light tackle meant it was excellent sport. Ling and conger were the other main target species, particularly during summer when, if the tides allowed, it was possible to drop the anchor and use fresh mackerel baits to tempt these hard-fighting predators.

On a memorable trip in August 2005, I was fortunate to grab a last-minute place when another club was looking for an extra person to make up the numbers. Arriving at the wreck when the tide was running hard, I set about catching a few pollock using tried and tested methods. As the tide slackened, down went the anchor, followed soon afterwards by a large mackerel bait on the end of my line. It wasn't down there long before I felt a very strong bite. Well, not so much a bite, more like the rod being pulled from my grip. Instinctively (I was quite good at this fishing lark by then!), I dropped the rod a little towards the fish, engaged the reel, and lifted in to a heavy fish. Conger eels fight very hard and it's important to get them moving up and away from the wreck before they get a chance to wrap their tail around any wreckage, or retreat inside the structure itself. I kept the pressure on and after a good tussle the unmistakable shape of an angry conger eel was at the side of the boat. Ever the attentive skipper, Roger was already stood beside me ready to deal with the fish. I calmly announced, "That's my first-ever conger", as an estimated 30 to 40 lb. of eel stared back at us.

Roger offered that we could wrestle it in to the boat for a photo, but I think it was a leading question! A conger eel thrashes around a lot and, apart from risking damage to itself, poses a hazard to anyone who gets in the way. Instead, we sensibly elected to release the fish at the side of the boat, with Roger expertly removing the hook from the eel as he had done a thousand times before, without bringing the eel on board. With a few powerful movements of its solid muscular body, my first-ever conger disappeared back into the depths. I followed up this eel with two smaller ones, before a large tope took my bait; a true bonus weighing in at 42 lb. on the boat, it remains my biggest-ever fish! It also needed no encouragement to distance itself from the boat as soon as it was released.

We caught a lot of fish on those wreck trips. I remember staggering up the pontoon from the boat one night with the first of several bags containing a total of 20 large pollock. "Serves him bloody right," was uttered by one of my fellow anglers with the usual big smiles, laughter and back slapping which went with the territory.

From June to December, the club's boat trips were competitions, and we fished a huge variety of marks. October to December would focus on fishing a short distance south of the Needles. Using large squid baits fished hard on the bottom in the often-fierce tides, the targets were the legendary Needles winter cod which could weigh over 40 lb. In October 2001, I managed to catch two Needles cod in the same day. With the fish weighing in at 18 lb. 5 oz. and 13 lb., my grin stretched from ear to ear, threatening to extend beyond the page edges of the *Angling Times*, the *Angler's Mail* and *Sea Angler* in which my photo appeared. However, my personal best cod, a cracking fish weighing in at 21 lb., was caught in December 2001, just two days before my 21st birthday.

Once again, I had managed to take advantage of a last-minute opportunity, and had joined an Isle of Wight-based angling club for the day. This was a classic "4 o'clock fish". It was often the case that, having not caught a cod all day, a subtle change in the tide, usually a bit of movement just after slack water, or slackening off after running hard, coincided with the onset of dusk when these fish began to move inshore to feed. Bang - the prize for persevering with big squid baits all day was a cracking cod on the deck.

There were also plenty of other fish around on the inshore marks at this time of year. Whiting were very tasty and could be caught in good numbers on light tackle around slack water. Catches were bolstered by loads of pout and dogfish, along with occasional conger, ling and rays. It was a great season to be fishing inshore and ideal for our points-based competition system, where points were awarded for different species based on their size and ease of capture, with extra points awarded for fish which exceeded the regional specimen weight.

Summer boat fishing trips offered a huge variety of options, from inshore bass fishing to plaice fishing off Ventnor on the Isle of Wight, and from smoothhound fishing in the Solent to targeting tope and rays on the offshore banks. And of course, there was Alderney, a beautiful little island in the Channel Islands, just off the coast of Cherbourg. When I was first there twenty years ago, the island had a timeless beauty which I hope still exists today.

With a stunning coastline, great food, and (usually!) good weather, the waters around Alderney were also stuffed with fish. I'm sure it will not surprise you to learn that my motive for going there was for the fishing! Luckily, I knew a man who could help. Roger ran regular trips to Alderney from

Lymington throughout the summer months and I was lucky enough to join two of these trips, in 1999 on Sundance II and in 2000 on Sundance. (Sundance II was replaced by the new and even-faster Sundance ready for the new millennium, and what a beauty she was! Sundance was an astonishing angling platform with a deck which felt big enough to host a game of five-a-side football. More speed meant a quicker journey out to the fishing marks, more time fishing and more fish on board.)

The fishing around Alderney was superb, with bass, brill and turbot the main target species, caught whilst drifting the numerous sandbanks with launce (big sandeels) or cut mackerel baits. So good was the fishing, in fact, that it was easy to think of it as normal after a couple of days. Yet, there aren't too many places around the UK where you could say, "Right, today we're going turbot fishing." In Alderney you could.

My first trip coincided with the total solar eclipse in August 1999 and, when it became obvious to the nation's press that Alderney was going to offer the best chance of seeing it, a whole load of reporters descended during the night, providing some logistical challenges on a very small island. I caught plenty of fish on that trip and learnt loads, so couldn't wait to go back the following year.

On the first day of the trip in 2000, we stopped briefly in mid Channel for a stretch of legs (there was a basking shark to watch) and to feather up a box full of mackerel before heading straight for the Alderney banks (that's sandbanks, not ones with a cash dispenser). Having left Lymington in the pouring rain, by the time we got to Alderney it was hot and flat calm and we were soaking up the sunshine, the way it stayed for the week. On that first afternoon we caught 79

17

bass and nine flatfish! This was phenomenal fishing and I personally contributed five bass and two brill, including my first ever, to the catch. My first turbot came the following day, and although I never achieved an "Alderney grand slam" of a bass, brill and turbot in the same day, it was not for lack of trying.

A bonus of these trips was that on the last day, it was often possible to fish a mid-Channel wreck on the way back to Lymington, perhaps using the flood tide to push us towards home, arriving on a wreck at slack water for more fishy mayhem. The banter on board (and on shore!) was relentless. The term "snowflake" hadn't been invented in those days and it was probably just as well. It was also fun to mix with skippers and crews from other south-coast ports, and we enjoyed fantastic hospitality from the local accommodation providers.

For me, the many fantastic boat trips I enjoyed over the years summed up what boat fishing was all about - having fun and enjoying some great fishing in good company. The weather would not always play ball, of course, and it was customary to ring in the night before a trip to see if it was going ahead. If it was too windy, the trip would be off. I know I am far from alone in saying that I looked forward to these boat trips in much the same way a small child looks forward to Christmas. They were brilliant times, and Roger was an incredible inspiration to me, always encouraging and willing to help. He also showed great interest in my progress over the years, from the 14-year-old on that first wreck trip right through to later trips when I was visiting home from university. Roger retired at the end of 2006, yet many years later much of what I learnt from him stills proves invaluable.

THE FAMOUS "RED-HOT KETTLE"

For Roger, each day was a new challenge, seeking out fish with a fresh crew and different weather to the previous day. I can definitely relate to this now, with each day in the mountains bringing a new group of clients and different weather conditions to contend with. Dealing with clients and treating them as customers was definitely something I remembered, as well as his continual ability to inspire confidence, and constantly juggle a huge number of tasks to ensure a fun, safe and successful trip. Looking back, it was also good, on occasions, to witness diplomacy in action, for example if an angler sought advice from Roger, ignored it and went their own sweet way, then blamed everyone but themselves for failing to catch! It was a privilege to fish with him and to learn so much, not only about fishing, from such an inspirational character.

I also remember very fondly Roger's confidence in my angling abilities, a lot of which he can take credit for, of course. I remember one particular wreck trip when an angler asked Roger casually, "Any tips, Rog?" Without hesitation, Roger simply replied, "Watch James, he is rather good at this!" Expressing some disbelief, based presumably on my youthful appearance, the angler clearly had some doubt. Roger's confidence in me was cemented by replying, "James has been doing this for years. He's been doing this bloody well for years."

It seems that Millie's comment, "You're quite good at this, James!" was absolutely right!

Chapter 3

Stars In The Sky

After my first wreck trip in 1995, I was looking forward to a summer in between schools, and with several years living in Lymington ahead of me, a lack of fishing wasn't going to be a problem.

Between 1995 and 1999, fishing was the centre of the universe as far as I was concerned, whilst school was a necessary evil. In fact, I frequently wondered whether it was necessary at all. Exams seemed nothing more than a memory test. Whenever in later life is it necessary to regurgitate a whole load of stuff about any particular subject? There are always resources at hand to help research a topic and references to any information used in a report or paper must always be cited appropriately. Even at school age, it seemed to me that coursework and research assignments carried far more relevance to future work experience than exams. I really didn't enjoy school at all, despite being an able pupil, viewing it as something of an intrusion when there were more exciting things to be doing, like fishing. This did begin to change a little when I got to the stage of doing my A-levels, but on balance, school was not for me.

Changing schools to start my GCSEs was tough because most children had already been at that school for three years, and were part of well-formed friendship groups. As an outsider, breaking in to any groups was difficult and wasn't something I found easy at all. There were some nice children in school but it took a while to work out who they were! Then there was the issue that, had I been at my new school from day 1, I would have been in the accelerated classes for subjects such as science and maths. Unfortunately, the timing of my arrival at my new school meant it was too late to slot in to these groups. It was only because some of the teachers worked tirelessly with me in their own time that I was able to catch up on what I had missed in the preceding year and progress. My success at school may therefore appear strange! However, I think my attitude was, "the harder I work, the quicker I'll be able to leave". Unfortunately, this was not the case and I was stuck with it.

On the plus side, outside of school I found each and every member of the fishing club made me very welcome. It turned out that sea fishing was very rewarding but also quite hard. In a lake, the fish are contained in a finite space, so it's just a case of finding them and working out how to catch them, albeit often easier said than done. In the sea, however, the fish may simply not be there. The sea is, to all intents and purposes, limitless, and with the huge seasonality of different species moving around our coast, and the impacts of the weather, even finding the fish can present a challenge. Flipping it around though, fish are predators, seeking an easy meal, so if you can put the right bait in the right place at the right time, you will catch them. That is the holy grail of angling.

The club had a very active junior section at that time, and this helped me find my feet with beach fishing. The club's junior summer league presented a perfect opportunity to get started, and it was very enjoyable, travelling to different venues and learning all the time. Much of the match fishing on the beaches was done at night, so my Christmas present that year was a headlamp, and I started to fish some of the monthly club shore competitions. Mid-week summer and winter league matches followed, and the monthly shingle bank league competitions. Whilst all this was going on, I was a regular on the club's monthly boat competitions. I was fishing a lot!

Hurst Castle had featured frequently in my childhood holidays, and became a place I visited many times whilst shore fishing. The castle was interesting historically, having been built by King Henry VIII between 1541 and 1544 as part of a chain of defences to protect ports and landing places in southern England from European invaders. Later, the captured King Charles I was held captive in the castle during the winter of 1648, not long before he was moved to London for trial and eventual execution, in January 1649.

The castle itself is situated on the end of a long spit of shingle beach, well over a mile long, projecting out into the main channel of the Solent. This spit is known to anglers simply as "the shingle bank". The seaward side of the shingle bank is exposed to the full force of the weather from the prevailing south-westerly winds, and can be truly frightening when enormous waves crash ashore, followed shortly afterwards by the deafening roar of the shingle grinding back down the beach in the backwash. Thankfully it was often a good deal less dramatic than this, and was a superb shore fishing venue. Behind the shingle bank is an altogether more tranquil scene, with a series of mudflats and river channels meandering their way across the salt marshes. These "backwaters", as anglers refer to them, are also good for fishing, albeit the species being targeted and the methods employed differ significantly between the seaward side of the shingle bank and the backwaters. The venue has been compared to a mini Chesil Beach, that enormous bank of shingle in Dorset stretching 18 miles from

Portland to West Bay, separating the English Channel from the Fleet, a shallow tidal lagoon.

There is a surprisingly large piece of land at the end of the shingle bank, and walking around the point from the seaward side to the backwaters is an interesting transition. At the end of the shingle bank you can walk around the front of the castle, past a series of groynes, soon reaching Hurst Hole, a particularly deep part of the sea very close to the beach. Continuing round and away from the castle leads to the altogether more tranquil beach facing the inner Solent and known as the back sand bar, which eventually meets the backwaters at the point where the river meets the inner Solent at the end of another mini shingle spit. The position of the main spit and the resultant narrowing, of the main channel of the Solent between Hurst Castle and the Isle of Wight, mean the tides in the area are fierce, so strong in fact that some areas can only be fished from the shore during certain parts of the tidal cycle. This makes it an interesting venue to fish as there are almost several venues in one. Depending on the times of high and low tide, the size of the tide, whether it was day or night, the time of year, and the weather, fishing a match there often meant fishing one spot for a couple of hours before moving somewhere else. I was fascinated by this, and learnt a huge amount about fishing the venue, partly by copying what others were doing, partly by listening to advice, and partly by my own trial and error.

Apart from the intricacies of trying to catch a few fish, of which there could be many across a whole range of species through the year, it was a beautiful spot to fish. On a still summer evening, the sound of curlews could be heard from across the mudflats, while there is something magical about the rhythm of the waves lapping the shore. Being a long way from the nearest settlement, it was very dark, so on a clear night there would be thousands of stars visible in the night sky. I was fascinated by three particularly recognisable stars, more or less evenly spaced in a straight line, which I now know to be Orion's Belt. Viewing it in the Northern Hemisphere during the winter months, this beautiful shape moved slowly and predictably across the clear night sky. My father and I referred to Orion's Belt as "my three stars". Enjoying an evening's fishing together these stars would often be visible and, in later life when we lived many miles apart, the sight of these stars still reminds us both of those happy nights on the beach. Many years later I would view Orion's Belt from high in the Himalayas, incredulous that the same stars I had viewed from the shingle bank, many thousands of miles away, were so distinctive and visible. My affinity and wonder for wild, remote places and the outdoors were very evident from an early age.

Amid this tranquillity, the area around the castle itself always had an atmosphere about it. If truth be told, it was quite an eerie place, and I always felt slightly uneasy in the immediate vicinity of the castle in the dead of night when I was on my own. I was not alone in this, and knew of more than one person in the fishing club who felt similarly, so we were always relieved (even if we didn't admit it) when it transpired that someone else had the same game plan in a match, and you could fish up at Hurst Castle together.

But why the atmosphere? I was well used to roaming around on beaches, alone in the dead of night. What was the difference? I think there is often an atmosphere in historic buildings, perhaps because of their age, or perhaps knowing of what happened there. Think of Hampton Court Palace or the Tower of London, for example. There had certainly been some strange goings-on reported at Hurst Castle. I remember being told a story of some engineers doing some work in the lighthouse which stood adjacent to the castle. It is reported that one night they downed tools for the day as usual and went home for the night. Returning for work the next day, the lighthouse had been locked from the *inside* overnight. On another occasion, my father and I witnessed a strange light moving along the top of the castle wall one night. The wall was inaccessible to anyone without a very long ladder. The area near the castle had even been the scene of a chilling and brutal murder in 1995. It is also reported that the captive King Charles I was allowed to walk along the spit for exercise during the time of his internment in the castle. At night, alone, it was certainly a creepy place.

The shingle bank will always be held fondly in my memories. However, it has to be said that the vast majority of places where I fished were very pleasant. Venues down in Dorset were particularly special, places such as Chesil Beach, Worbarrow Bay, Lulworth Cove and Portland Breakwater. Hampshire was very much "home turf", and it would be quite hard to think of a beach or piece of shoreline along the Hampshire coastline which I have never set foot on! It was also lovely to fish further afield occasionally, for example in Sussex at Pevensey Bay and at Pagham, and at several venues on the Isle of Wight.

I think it is fair to say I was a popular member of the sea fishing club. I had arrived as a keen-as-mustard 14-year-old, with lots of enthusiasm but not much knowledge. I listened to everyone who freely offered their advice and I kept my eyes and ears open. I was not scared of being beaten in matches (which was most of the time initially!) and it turned out that often, it was the nights when everyone caught more than me that I learnt the most because I remembered next time.

As the months rolled on and turned in to years, I wasn't a young lad anymore, but a young man. A moment which brought me down to earth with a bump was when I turned 17 and became too old to be classed as a junior anymore, so was up against all the adults. These adults included some incredibly talented anglers, with years of experience and stacks of local knowledge. Our club was home to several regulars in the various England teams, including the legendary Chris Clark, a former world shore angling champion. Fishing alongside anglers of this calibre helped put perspective on things - this was the standard to strive for, and I persevered and fished, fished, and fished. Hours and hours went in to my preparations - preparing rigs, digging bait, studying tide tables and weather forecasts, and eventually I started to get placed in matches, both shore and boat, and went on to win several competitions.

I owe a huge debt of gratitude to the many wonderful friends I made in the Lymington and District Sea Fishing Club, who taught me so much and gave me so many lifts around before I passed my driving test. Happily I am still in touch with many of them now.

Chapter 4

Cardiff And The Caribbean

Cardiff is a great city. For me to claim a city as great, it must be pretty special, being far more at home in the wilds of Scotland or on some deserted beach in the middle of nowhere. The capital of Wales, Cardiff is Wales' chief commercial centre, the base for many Welsh cultural and media institutions, and the seat of the National Assembly for Wales, the devolved parliament of Wales since 1999. Cardiff has a rich industrial heritage, having been the main port for coal export from South Wales through the mid-1800s. The town, as it was then, grew rapidly at this time. Despite competition from the development of Barry Docks from the 1880s, Cardiff continued to flourish. At its coal exchange, where the price of coal on the British market was determined, the first million-pound deal was struck in 1907. Cardiff was granted city status in 1905 by King Edward VII but, sadly, the docks entered a prolonged decline after the First World War. By 1936, their trade was less than half its value in 1913, reflecting the slump in demand for Welsh coal. Cardiff was recognised as the Welsh capital from 1955, yet it was not until the 1980s and onwards into the new millennium that Cardiff has enjoyed major redevelopment and investment, particularly in the area around Cardiff Bay. These days, Cardiff is a significant and multicultural European city, a major tourist destination and an important cultural, political, academic, sporting and industrial centre.

In addition to the establishment of the National Assembly for Wales, 1999 was a great year for Cardiff. For starters, Wales was the principal host of the Rugby

World Cup that year. Rugby runs in the veins of the Welsh and Cardiff's Millennium Stadium was buzzing on the day of the final between Australia and France. Australia won the tournament and I was there, albeit sadly outside the stadium, to witness the arrival of Her Majesty The Queen. However, even more significantly than that, a clever boy who loved fishing was about to embark on his undergraduate career at Cardiff University. The crowds welcoming me easily rivalled those outside the Millennium Stadium on the day of the Rugby World Cup final. Well, perhaps not, but once across the River Severn there was a sign next to the M4 announcing, "*Croeso i Gymru*" (Welcome to Wales).

It was the autumn of 1999. I had completed my GCSEs and A-levels, and had been working at weekends and during the school holidays in a local supermarket for the past couple of years. This was to fund my fishing and help during my time at university. My A-levels were in biology, chemistry, maths, further maths, and general studies, which meant mostly I was doing maths homework, fitting in the other subjects around that. Often a weekend would involve working in the supermarket on Friday night and all day Saturday, then fishing a shore competition on Saturday night before a boat trip on Sunday. Fitting in learning to drive and school work with mid-week evening fishing competitions and bait digging was good practice for juggling later in life.

Just days before heading off to university, I fished a match at Southbourne one night. As ever, I had put in the leg-work, digging plenty of fresh lugworms to target the expected flatfish on this relatively shallow, sandy venue. By the end of the night I had caught three soles and a dab, enough to win the competition and send me off to start my university days on a high. Thankfully, I was able to continue fishing through the university holidays and on occasional weekends when I went home.

I spent three very happy years at Cardiff University between 1999 and 2002, studying ecology. One of the appeals of their biological sciences degree schemes was that they shared a common first year before specialising in subsequent years. So for example, you could enrol for a generic "biology" degree initially, yet end up pursuing a degree in ecology, zoology or genetics, based on how your interests developed over the common first year. Further specialisation was possible at the end of the second year, so ultimately, I was able to tailor the degree to my strengths and interests of freshwater ecology, fish biology and statistics. My distinct dislike for school all changed when I went to Cardiff and I loved the learning, the research and the social life. The academics were among the most motivating people I had ever met, and I couldn't help but strive to emulate them in some small way. Indeed, my entire impression of the British education system had improved drastically for me when I was able to make "fish" the subject of the entire curriculum!

My final year was made up of several modules, one of which was a field course held in the summer holiday before the final year started. One of the options was to go to Tobago and carry out surveys and studies of fish behaviour on the coral reefs. It would have been rude not to. Tobago is an interesting little island and although "Trinidad and Tobago" is frequently spoken of as a single entity, Tobago is very different to Trinidad. One of the differences is that Tobago has coral reefs. Trinidad, situated closer to the coast

29

of South America than Tobago, is subjected to a lot of silt and suspended sediments coming from the great Orinoco River in Venezuela, meaning the water around Trinidad is not suitable for coral. Tobago, on the other hand, sits well away from the river mouth and enjoys lovely clear water.

The field course was hard work (honestly!) Far harder, however, was convincing people it was hard work when we got home. Indeed, that's when the real work started, analysing and writing up all the data. Based out of Charlotteville in the north of the island, the field course was two weeks long. Luckily, all my fellow students and I (21 of us altogether, if I remember correctly) arranged to stay on for a further week to explore the rest of the island and generally enjoy a bit of a holiday. I had only spent two weeks in the sea, surrounded by fish, so after a day spent moving to another part of the island for our group holiday, I was getting fishy withdrawal symptoms. I looked up a local charter fishing boat skipper and enjoyed a great couple of days fishing for barracuda on the shallow reefs. You don't get many barracuda in the Solent, so that made a nice change. We saw some magical sunsets too but, lovely as they were, being in the tropics they didn't last very long. At 6 p.m. it would be broad daylight, then it would be pitch black by 6:30 p.m. - nowhere near as wonderful as the endless summer sunsets of Scotland's northwest that I would enjoy in future! It was a touch warmer though.

Tobago was one of many wonderful experiences I have enjoyed over the years, and the sort of trip which made working in the supermarket during the university holidays so worthwhile. Our tunes for the trip were Shaggy's *Angel* and Moby's *Why Does My Heart Feel So Bad?* These songs still take me straight back to the Caribbean whenever I hear them.

I made some very good friends during my undergraduate days and thoroughly enjoyed myself. On Wednesday nights, *Jive Hive* in the Students' Union's own nightclub promised a particularly classy opportunity to enjoy the best of '70s, '80s and '90s classics, with the likes of A-ha's *Take On Me* and Bon Jovi's *Livin' On A Prayer* ensuring the dance floor stayed jumping well into the small hours. In fact, so sticky with spilt beer was the dance floor that continuing to move on it (I hesitate to use the word "dance") was the only way to prevent your shoes sticking to the floor.

However, one of the best nights in Cardiff was shared with Fiona when we went to see R.E.M. in the Millennium Stadium some years later. It was a fantastic concert, and when the opening chords of *Everybody Hurts* kicked in, Fiona and I both looked at each other and said, in a satisfied manner, "Great, we can go home after this." That has always been a special song for us, and Michael Stipe did not disappoint. This particular song was all the more poignant as the concert was taking place shortly after the July 2005 terrorist bombing attacks in London. Of course we stayed to the very end, in the sweltering heat, with our new black (perfect for a hot summer) R.E.M. T-shirts soaked with sweat. At "chucking-out time", Fiona and I held hands for fear of losing each other in the thousands of people now pouring from the stadium and made our way back to the car. We couldn't hear for at least a week afterwards - a sure sign of a good concert.

My supermarket job from school days continued throughout my time as an undergraduate and the shop welcomed me back full-time every holiday. These periods coincided with all their busy times, namely Christmas, Easter and the summer, so this arrangement suited both parties. Working in a supermarket on December 23rd, traditionally the busiest trading day of the year, is something everybody should experience at least once in their life! I worked like a Trojan through the holidays, which funded me through the following term, ultimately resulting in no student debt. Result!

I was delighted to graduate with a First Class Honours degree in 2002. A PhD opportunity had presented itself, still with Cardiff University, to start in the autumn of 2002. Surprisingly, it was going to involve fish, so I was quite happy. Indeed, anyone who knew me up until this point in my life would have been very surprised if my next move had *not* involved fish. As you may have realised by now, I loved fish and was mad keen on fishing, so it seemed as sensible a thing to do as anything, to turn my passion into my job. My love for fish and fishing was about to become a fledging academic research career. It would become ironic later that chasing this career took me to Scotland, and the mountains. But for now, I skipped back home to Lymington with a big cheesy grin on my face and a decent degree in my back pocket. I worked in the supermarket all summer to get some money in the bank and fished as much as I could, without a care in the world.

Chapter 5

Dr. Fish

I was thrilled to be offered the PhD studentship, but it meant a big change for me. I would be enrolled as a student at Cardiff University. However, the practical work and the majority of my time, nine months or so a year, was to be in Scotland, with just a couple of months a year in Cardiff. I would be working in collaboration with what was then the Fisheries Research Services (FRS) Freshwater Laboratory in Pitlochry. (FRS was an Executive Agency of the Scottish Government. From 1st April 2009, FRS became part of Marine Scotland, part of the core Scottish Government.) This was exciting, but scary at the same time. I loved my fish, and I had done well with the research elements of my first degree. This was an excellent opportunity to train as a scientific researcher in a field I loved. However, the reality was that I had to leave everything I knew, and after spending just a week in Cardiff to enrol and sort logistics, I packed my computer and clothes into my trusty little red Nissan Micra and headed up the M6. The healthy English/Scots banter which would ensue never bothered me - I had got well used to the equally healthy English/Welsh banter at the time of the Five Nations Championship rugby tournament in 1999. (This was to become the Six Nations Championship from 2000.)

At the end of the summer, shortly before leaving Lymington to embark on my PhD, I left my supermarket job for the last time. There would be no university holidays now. I also fished a match at Hurst Castle one night and weighed in my best-ever bag of fish in a shore competition. With a catch of eleven pout, six black bream and two eels for a total weight of 11 lb. 3 oz., that was one heavy bucket to carry all the way back along the shingle bank. I finished the match in second place behind an exceptionally talented and hugely respected local angler, who, incidentally, doubled my weight with a good bag of scad! It was odd, however, to know that I would be fishing very little from now on. This was a very different feeling to after my success at Southbourne a few years previously, when I had won a match shortly before starting my undergraduate career. Then, I had known I would still be fishing reasonably frequently, making the most of the university holidays and occasional weekends when I went home. In fact, I had enjoyed quite a bit of success over that period. However, now moving to Scotland for most of the year, I would make it down to Lymington far less than I had done during my undergraduate days, meaning far less fishing. This PhD had better be good, I thought. Was it a mistake to pursue this career, knowing I was turning my passion into my work, which was, ironically, leading me away from my fishing?

I was about to eat, sleep and dream salmon for three years, metaphorically at least, so it was probably just as well I found them to be fascinating creatures. They had fins and lived in water. That was a good starting point, as far as I was concerned, and my interest was already kindled. Yet, that was about the extent of my salmon knowledge, leaving plenty of space on the back of the proverbial postage stamp for the weekly shopping list. Fortunately, my knowledge was about to increase dramatically.

Atlantic salmon display an anadromous life cycle, a posh way of saying they spawn in fresh water and the main feeding and growth phase occurs at sea. Spawning takes place during winter in clean, cold, well-oxygenated flowing water with a gravel bottom. Eggs are laid into a depression in the gravel by a female. After the eggs have been fertilised by a male or males, they are buried and begin to develop immediately. The eggs hatch in the spring and the young alevins remain in the gravel and feed from their yolk reserve. When this yolk reserve is almost entirely depleted, the young fish, now known as fry, emerge from the gravel and begin feeding independently. The fish then typically spend one or two years in fresh water, feeding on drifting invertebrates, and are known as parr throughout this period. Eventually, the time approaches for these parr to migrate downstream to sea. As they go, their bodies undergo a series of changes to equip them for life at sea. They are now known as smolts. Silvery in colour, smolts migrate in large numbers during spring. Once at sea, fish swim to rich feeding grounds in the North Atlantic Ocean, typically near Greenland and the Faroe Islands, where, feeding on large zooplankton and small fishes, they achieve a large size. After spending between one and four years at sea, adults return to the coast then migrate up their natal river to the area where they hatched previously, and so the life cycle begins again. Most fish die after spawning, but some survive and return to the sea as kelts, possibly to spawn another year.

My subject of study was the sheltering behaviour of Atlantic salmon. During the parr stage of their life cycle, Atlantic salmon use spaces between stones ("interstitial habitat") as refuges or shelters. This behaviour was thought to be an important aspect of their ecology, with applied interest for fisheries management purposes, yet relatively little was known about it - until I came along! Those years spent searching beneath stones for bullheads might now pay off, I thought. It seemed my knowledge of pollock and cod sheltering behind a wreck might come in handy at last.

I lived in Perth for the duration of my PhD. This was a convenient base as it was near the field station at Almondbank, where my day-to-day research work was carried out. Over the next three years I carried out several studies using a glass-sided indoor stream channel in conjunction with field work in local streams. The field station made an excellent base and I also benefitted from regular visits to the main laboratory in Pitlochry. It was a pretty lonely time all told, as it was a long way removed from a more traditional university-based research project, with the friends and social life which go with it, but the work itself was interesting and very self-generating - the more I applied myself, the better it went.

Safely settled in Scotland, I was now glad finally to have the opportunity to begin exploring Scotland's mountains.

Looking back, it seems I hadn't really stopped since I went to school when I was five years old. I had done well academically up to this point, gaining excellent GSCE and A-level results at school, and then a top result in my first degree. Yet, this had meant fully committing to all the work associated with those achievements. At the same time, I had been completely obsessed with my fishing, often being out midweek and at weekends. Juggling this with a weekend and holiday job, and other things such as learning to drive, I had packed quite a lot in. It would be good to escape to the mountains now I had some time to myself.

From my holidays in the Lake District as a child, I knew I enjoyed being amongst the mountains. However, there is a big difference between doing something when you have to do it, and doing something of your own free will. I knew Scotland would be a beautiful country, and I wasn't disappointed. I had funding for the three years of the PhD, but after that, who knew? Piecing together a career in scientific research has always relied upon being able to string together different research grants one after another, so if I was to stay working in research, I knew that my time in Scotland may well come to an end after three years. With this in mind, I decided to explore Scotland as much as possible in the relatively limited time I had available, just in case I moved on to pastures new at the end of my PhD.

So off I went. I bought myself a couple of maps and headed off, usually on both days of the weekend. My very first walk in the Scottish hills was a plod up onto some of the hills accessed from Glen Almond, and I remember seeing a large herd of red deer running away across the high and desolate moor. It was a wonderful place to be. A week later, in early November, I got a bit more adventurous, and drove up to the Linn of Dee near Braemar in the Cairngorms. I walked along Glen Lui up to Derry Lodge, before continuing westwards along Glen Luibeg. I stopped for lunch above the Luibeg Bridge, staring up at the slopes of Carn a' Mhaim with the first snows of the winter beginning to establish themselves beneath the ashen clouds. To the north, the cliffs of Coire Sputan Dearg were appearing and disappearing sporadically in the clouds. I was completely mesmerised by the scene around me. What struck me was the scale of everything. Not necessarily what I could actually see in front of me, but an awareness of the much greater environment around me. According to the map, it was telling what a short distance I had actually walked, yet all around me for many miles were a great sprawl of contour lines. The glens were beautiful, and I even spotted the occasional red deer, yet the tops looked quite uninviting that day, even when I could see them! Over subsequent years, I was to become very familiar with this area. But for now, I vowed I would return in the better weather come spring.

I did exactly that and, on one day in late March the following year, I headed back to Derry Lodge, but this time I headed north up Glen Derry before turning up past the Hutchison Memorial Hut and so to Loch Etchachan. This was my first visit to Loch Etchachan, and I was spellbound.

Loch Etchachan is a stunning spot, higher than many peaks in England and Wales, yet nestling in a bowl amid the great peaks of Beinn Mheadhoin, Derry Cairngorm and Ben Macdui, the spectacular scenery of the central Cairngorms. It was simply magnificent. Indeed, it came as something of a surprise when the loch suddenly appeared before me. Having climbed steeply from the Hutchison Memorial Hut, my arrival at the obvious flattening seemed rather abrupt. March is still winter in the Cairngorms, and today was no different. I only had a cheap pair of walking boots at the time, which had been fine to get me this far, but would not have taken me any higher that day. Great sheets of hard re-frozen snow-ice (*névé*) covered the surrounding peaks and slopes, and in future I would love to come and take advantage of such wonderful conditions. If I had been mesmerised in Glen Luibeg last November, today was beyond description. It felt other worldly. I was a long way from the car. In fact, I was a long way from anywhere. It is a full 17-mile round trip from the Linn of Dee to here, whilst to get here from any other direction would involve some pretty big distances across some very high ground.

Loch Etchachan was to become somewhere I would visit time and time again. Sometimes I would just plod up there and back, particularly in my early days of exploring the area, if the weather was poor. Sometimes I would climb Ben Macdui as an "out-and-back" from the Linn of Dee, a short day of just 21 miles! If I was feeling particularly fit, I might drop back to Loch Etchachan after first climbing Carn a' Mhaim and Ben Macdui, returning to Derry Lodge via Derry Cairngorm. Sometimes it was Beinn Mheadhoin which was the day's objective. It's no wonder I worry about what state my knees will be in when I'm older. In fact, it took a while for me to figure out that the gentle slopes leading up from Loch Etchachan eventually took you to the rim of the cliffs of Coire Sputan Dearg, those cliffs I had first spied in the November of the previous year.

Loch Etchachan will always be a very special place to me for another reason - I took my mother and father there on one day in May 2006. They did brilliantly, although the amount of snow up there surprised them a little. Winter holds on late up there. However, aside from the obvious pleasure of sharing a wonderful day out with people whom you love, my whole world had almost fallen apart late in 2003 when my mother had been diagnosed with cancer. I will always remember the phone call from Kate telling me the news. It was the sort of phone call when you knew something was very wrong as soon as she started speaking. This was terrifying news, particularly knowing that her dear mother had died of cancer at a similar age. Both my sisters were abroad and I was up in Scotland, but we all dropped everything and headed straight back to Lymington to help out my father with things whilst my mother was in hospital. A traumatic operation was followed by chemotherapy and radiotherapy and, thanks to the truly wonderful work of the National Health Service (NHS) and her incredible determination to survive, my mother is still with us today. Prior to this, I had often wondered, "How do you get through a time like this?" I'm not sure there is a right way or a wrong way, and it goes without saying that it was a hideous time for us all, but as a family we pulled together and just got on with what needed to be done. Perhaps it is better to deal with such things by keeping busy, or perhaps we didn't want to consider what might actually happen. Somehow, we did get through it, and as well as Loch Etchachan, I have taken my mother to the top of many lovely mountains over the years - Robinson, Hindscarth, Dale Head, Haystacks, Causey Pike, Grisedale Pike, Blencathra, Sail, Bleaberry Fell, High Seat, Maiden Moor, High Spy and Cat Bells in the Lake District, and Cairn Gorm, Morrone (Braemar), Meall a' Bhuachaille and Ben Vrackie in Scotland. But that day at Loch Etchachan was very special. Indeed, the timeless beauty of that special place means, when my parents are no longer with us, I shall be able to return to Loch Etchachan and will always remember them there.

Over the next couple of years I explored several areas, notably parts of the Cairngorms, the Angus Glens and parts of the central Highlands, even enjoying occasional forays to the west coast. I also picked up a book about the Munros, the Scottish mountains over 3,000 ft. It was great fun, getting out in the fresh air and exploring some amazing mountains and landscapes. I'm sure the weather was better than it is now, almost twenty years later. I was restricted to weekends, yet I do not remember the gales on the tops which seem to be so normal these days. Or perhaps this is just my mind tricking me as I get older? It seems to be human nature to remember fond memories in the sunshine.

My PhD was coming to an end. It was the spring of 2005 and I was looking at completing my last season of practical work before heading to Cardiff from mid-June to finish writing my thesis. I was spurred on by the fact that due to a series of events which tumbled nicely in my favour, there was an opening for a post-doctoral research associate coming up. This would be a move away from salmon to look at fish shoaling behaviour - a research post working for Cardiff University in collaboration with the University of St. Andrews and the FRS Freshwater Laboratory. In short, it would be a similar logistical setup to my PhD, working at the same field station/laboratory, but living permanently in Scotland. I jumped at the chance.

The summer passed incredibly quickly as I was under pressure to finish my PhD thesis and start my new post-doc on time. Although I spent most of the summer in Cardiff working on my thesis, I also managed to visit Lymington and enjoyed some much-needed quality time with my parents. I also took part in some of the last sea fishing trips I would ever do. A memorable evening at Paddy's Gap springs to mind, catching a lovely pair of smoothhounds for third place in a match. I always think smoothhounds are an evolutionist's favourite fish - a small and attractive member of the shark family, these sleek fish are incredibly powerful and have a terrific turn of speed, yet feed predominantly on crabs, not the fastest prey items in the sea! There was also that wonderful wreck trip when I caught my first-ever conger and a 42 lb. tope.

I am sure it is obvious that fishing and everything associated with it had been a huge part of my life over the previous decade or so. Yet, the "fishing" era of my life was coming to an end. In one sense it is sad that I never made a conscious decision to give it up, especially as there had been more to it than simply an activity I loved. It was a great time of my life when I was growing up and beginning to branch out into the world around me. The people I fished with were very special and extremely helpful to me, and they watched me develop from a keen young lad into a capable and competent beach and boat angler. I had been inspired by some of the best practitioners of their crafts and ultimately I had turned my passion for fish and fishing into a subject of study and then work, despite my earlier dislike for school. It felt entirely natural to be progressing into a career which built on my early passion in life, yet things were changing as the appeal of Scotland was certainly not just for my work.

I was very excited about the prospect of returning to Scotland, and the mountains, and to top it all I would now be earning enough money to rent a small flat all on my own. Come the autumn, I jumped back into my little red Nissan Micra which, by now, knew its own way up the M6. I slotted straight back into life in Scotland, starting my new post-doc and reacquainting myself with the good folk at the field station. The one slight snag was that, almost inevitably, my thesis was not quite complete, so during my first month back in Scotland I worked on my post-doc during the day, went home for tea, then worked on my thesis until 5 a.m. before grabbing a couple of hours' sleep. I would then get up and do it all over again, day after day, and night after night. I was shattered, physically and mentally, and the nature of writing a thesis is such that it becomes incredibly difficult ever to switch off, certainly mentally. Tag codes and Excel formulae were constantly whizzing around in my head, and I could quote great chunks of the relevant literature, such was my attention to detail in doing the best job I possibly could. However, finish it I did, and it was a proud day when I handed in my PhD thesis at Cardiff University. I completed my thesis examination in January 2006, and happily, had just a few minor corrections to make in order to be awarded my second degree. I was now a Doctor of Philosophy, or simply as Fiona entitled me, "Dr. Fish".

Returning eagerly to Scotland and the mountains, I was excited now to focus fully on my first post-doc. At that point, I was pretty much convinced I would be heading down the route of carving out a career as a research scientist in the academic world. Indeed, as much as I loved being in the mountains, I didn't realise it was even possible to make a living out of taking folk out in the hills. Yet, it is ironic that if I hadn't gone to Scotland to do a PhD in the first place, I may never have started exploring the mountains. My initial thoughts, that I should make the most of the opportunity to explore Scotland as much as possible over the past three years, had turned into the realisation that Scotland, and more specifically Scotland's mountains, was where I wanted to be. This was a true turning point.

Chapter 6

Morocco - Mules And Mountains

With my PhD safely in the bag and my first post-doc going well, life was looking good. I had funding until June 2007, still over a year away, and was enjoying the combined benefits of a university research job whilst living in a beautiful area close to the mountains. My flat was in the village of Stanley, just north of Perth, and was a perfect springboard for weekend adventures in the hills to the east, north and west.

One thing which quickly dawned on me was that winter on Scotland's mountains was not to be trifled with. It is no exaggeration that conditions on Scotland's mountains during winter are Arctic, with storm-force winds, sub-zero temperatures and blizzards entirely normal. "Whiteout" conditions, when clouds descend on totally snow-covered terrain leading to conditions of zero visibility, are another norm. There are also specific snow hazards such as cornices (overhanging masses of snow which form on the lee side of ridges and plateau edges) and the risk of avalanches. Suddenly, the Scottish mountains in winter start to sound like a scary place to be. Even in summer, it is typically colder, wetter and windier in the mountains than at sea level, catching out the unwary if not suitably equipped.

Many years later, it became obvious to me that visitors to Scotland can grossly underestimate the severity of conditions on the mountains, especially in winter. Particularly among visitors from overseas, it seems the relatively low heights of the Scottish mountains in a worldwide context can lead to a somewhat scornful view of their seriousness. Yet, Scotland sits at quite a high northerly latitude, comparable with parts of Canada, albeit generally warmer thanks to the effect of the Gulf Stream. Furthermore, Scotland is subjected to the full force and variability of weather systems originating from the Atlantic Ocean, the Arctic and Scandinavia, none of which win any "sunniest place in the world" awards. It can be surprisingly difficult to convince someone they really should carry a hat and gloves with them in the middle of summer when going up a Scottish mountain. Even more curious is the fact that carrying, and frequently wearing, ski goggles is often absolutely essential in winter, yet this is often questioned by those with little experience. Recently, having had clients repeatedly turn up without them, my diplomacy skills progressed from simply having them on the kit list, to having them on the kit list in bold type, before finally having them on the kit list in capitalized bold type. This was all to no avail, so I have since gone out and bought ski goggles for my clients to borrow. You cannot see anything when a 50 mph Cairngorms "breeze" is blowing snow straight in your face and freezing your eyelashes. Indeed, it is often commented that if you can survive in Scotland's mountains in winter you can survive anywhere in the world. Certainly many world-class mountaineers have started their careers in Scotland and gone on to magnificent achievements in the greater ranges. No, you don't mess around in the Scottish mountains, particularly in winter.

With the likelihood of winter on Scotland's high mountains extending from November through to April as a minimum, I didn't like the idea of hanging up my walking boots in October with the possibility of their not seeing the light of day again until the following May. Far better to embrace winter, I thought, and learn some of the essential skills which would keep me safe through all seasons, so I enrolled on a winter skills course. This was to be my first formal instruction, and little did I know that I would eventually be running my own! I opted for a two-day course because I thought, "If I don't like it, I'm sure I can put up with two days."

I loved every minute of the course. We covered many of the skills which I now teach routinely, such as moving on snow-covered terrain, crampon and ice axe skills, navigation, avalanche awareness, weather forecasts, planning a winter day out, emergency procedures, kit selection etc. Winter skills, like anything in life, need to be practised and honed. I knew I wasn't going to become a snow Jedi overnight so practice, experience and developing judgement were now required. I had recognised two things: firstly, this winter lark opens up a whole new world, both at home and abroad; and secondly, there are people, just like the instructor on my first course, who work in Scotland's mountains and make a living from it. The instructor had seemed so keen, so enthusiastic about her group for the weekend, so encouraging and so capable when it came to dealing with conditions in a rapidly changing and serious mountain environment. Interesting, I thought; that would be a fabulous way to earn a living!

Winter 2006/2007 came and went, and with it some excellent winter hill days. Experience gained in Scotland can sometimes be on the wrong side of scary, but if you can survive the epics and learn from them, so much the better! A rare bluebird day towards the end of March 2007 provided a fine day out on Sgurr Eilde Mor and Binnein Mor in the Mamores, yet the superb spring conditions still required careful negotiation of a bullet-hard and heavily corniced summit ridge on Binnein Mor.

* * * * * *

Come spring 2007, I travelled to Morocco for the first time. This was a little treat as I fancied doing something abroad that was a bit different. At this time, I didn't really have any financial worries. Thanks to my hard work in the supermarket during my undergraduate days, I had completed my first degree without debt and my PhD had been funded so was cost-neutral. Although I had no savings, I was single, I lived in a modest rented flat and my idea of fun was heading to the hills with a few sandwiches. My outgoings were modest and I was working hard, so why not?

I also love travel and one of the things I enjoyed about the academic world was the opportunity to visit different countries, for example to attend conferences or to work collaboratively with other institutions. I had been to some interesting places via this route and it was often possible to tag a few days on at the end of a trip to do a bit of independent exploring. All told, I have visited Tobago, Iceland, Sweden, Canada, Denmark, France, Ireland and several states in the USA via my scientific work, and have undertaken personal trips to Slovakia, Germany, Tenerife, Morocco, Nepal, Bolivia, Israel, Iceland and Norway. Travel is a great way of broadening the mind and exploring different cultures and places. Aside from the enjoyable experiences I had at the time, these travel experiences were to serve me well later in life when my clients were typically not Aviemore residents, or even from Scotland or the UK, but may have come from anywhere in the world. (Aviemore is a village in the Highlands of Scotland in an area known as Speyside, where I live.) It seems that experienced travellers from across the globe appreciate my breadth of travel experience and general knowledge of other places when it comes to enriching their time in Scotland.

Morocco turned out to be a true delight. Accessible in less than four hours from London by plane, yet the culture is so very different from anything in Europe. Marrakech, one of Morocco's four imperial cities and its former capital, provided my first taste of Morocco. At least 1,000 years old, Marrakech became significant during the 11th century and it was around this time that the first Koutoubia mosque was built. The minaret, of later date, still dominates the Marrakech skyline, which is very handy if you get lost! The city is divided into two parts: the Medina, which is the old part within the medieval ramparts, and Gueliz, the more modern French quarter. There are two absolute highlights of any visit to Morocco within the Medina. Firstly, the mysterious souk, a myriad alleyways and small shops selling leather goods, spices, rugs, tasty local food and a whole host of other things. It is incredibly easy to get lost in there. Secondly, and adjacent to the souk, is the famous square, the Djemaa el Fna, the meeting place of the dead. Thankfully the thousands of people I saw meeting there were very much alive, but what a sensory overload. During the day the square is busy enough, but come night time, the whole place is buzzing with snake charmers, fire eaters, dancers, fortune tellers and many stalls selling local snacks. If the throng is a little too much to take in, there are some lovely calm cafés with terraces overlooking the square from which to observe the goings-on. The Djemaa el Fna must surely boast the highest density of cobras anywhere in the world, while a local gentleman selling dentures from a stall reminded me why it is a good idea to have a dental check before travelling!

Our itinerary was for a relaxed week-long trek in to the High Atlas Mountains, attempting to climb Ouanoukrim (4,088 m), Morocco's second highest peak, and Toubkal (4,167 m), the highest mountain in the whole of North Africa.

Leaving Marrakech, we drove to the small town of Imlil at the end of the road accessible to motor vehicles, heading in to the High Atlas. A busy place, it buzzes with the toing and froing associated with groups starting and finishing treks into the mountains. I was travelling as part of an organised trip with several locals working alongside our group's leader. A fascinating aspect of being amongst the local population was the observance of the Islamic call to prayer five times daily. With the first of those at dawn, getting up early wasn't a problem. Winter is a wonderful time to be in these high mountains. Like Scotland, they have seasonal snows only in the winter, so there are no glaciers to worry about. This was, however, going to be my first taste of climbing at an altitude of over 4,000 m. Given the height of the peaks we aimed to climb, it was important to take acclimatisation seriously.

Acclimatisation is the process by which the body adapts to reduced oxygen availability at a specific altitude. As you climb higher, air pressure decreases, meaning the oxygen molecules in the air are further apart. The result is fewer oxygen molecules in a given volume of air and therefore less oxygen available for the body to use. It is therefore vital to act accordingly whenever venturing above 2,500 m, taking a gradual ascent to allow the body to adapt (or acclimatise) to this lack of oxygen.

I was a little nervous about this as Scotland's mountains can prepare you for many things, but climbing at high altitude is not one of them. It is very difficult to know how you will respond to the effects of altitude without trying the hard way. Fortunately, most reasonably fit and healthy people are perfectly capable of acclimatising to this sort of altitude and higher, provided they take some precautions. The essential thing is to avoid going too high too fast, and the whole process of acclimatisation is aided greatly by drinking plenty of fluids. Some mild symptoms of altitude sickness, such as a mild headache, nausea and shortage of breath, are to be expected until you have acclimatised. More severe symptoms are a definite warning sign to retreat to a lower altitude immediately. Mild altitude sickness can easily become more serious if ignored, leading to complications with the brain and lungs, which can ultimately lead to death.

Thankfully, taking the necessary precautions seemed to work quite well for me and despite a mild headache for a time, I didn't suffer any serious effects. It's amazing what you can do if you listen to your leader. I was certainly hill fit, having put in the days in Scotland before leaving, but had to balance this against the need to slow things down the higher we went. Age, sex and physical fitness do not affect the likelihood of getting altitude sickness. Rushing (or more accurately, trying to rush) is not a good idea at altitude. On later trips, venturing to over 6,000 m in the Himalayas and the Andes, this early experience was to prove vital, particularly with regards to understanding that any ascent must be broken up into sections - allowing the body to acclimatise to a new normal before attempting to move higher.

We started our trek from Imlil with a short stroll towards our overnight accommodation in Aroumd, a village a short distance further up the valley. This accommodation was fairly luxurious, having electricity, showers and toilets! It also had stunning views of the nearby mountains, covered in snow on their upper slopes and rising steeply from the valley floor. The eating area was very cosy with its roaring log fire, and it was very easy to fall asleep in there after a lovely dinner, curling up on the comfy seats in a down jacket.

Eating and drinking is a really important part of any trip abroad. This suits me down to the ground. From a cultural perspective, it is an important aspect of the overall experience. Wherever I have travelled, I have found that the local people take a great pride in their country, its food, culture and traditions, and tend to be extremely good hosts. Morocco was no different and the friendly and welcoming Berber people of the High Atlas Mountains were obviously and rightly very proud of their beautiful country. We enjoyed some thoroughly good food, including the Moroccan classic *tajine* - mutton and vegetable stew cooked in a traditional earthenware pot. *Cous-cous* was also frequently enjoyed with this, and I remember the excellent home-baked bread as well as occasional chicken and lots of aubergines. Morocco is also one of the world's largest sardine exporters so there was some delicious oily fish to enjoy. Mint tea is the staple Moroccan drink and, as well as being very refreshing, it added variety to the drinks menu as we were drinking plenty of water to aid acclimatisation. However, as well as showing appreciation for your hosts, eating and drinking is important for your overall well-being whilst trekking. Even in Aroumd we were already at an altitude of nearly 2,000 m, and the nights were cold. Walking day after day and expending lots of energy to keep moving, and even just to keep warm, requires a high calorie intake. And you wonder why I love mountaineering so much?!

With a hearty breakfast inside us, our first full trekking day was an acclimatisation walk up to a nearby viewpoint, returning to Aroumd the same day. This has the effect of tricking your body into thinking you are higher than you really are, so your body works harder to deal with it.

The following day we left Aroumd and headed up the valley and into the heart of the mountains. We were now joined by a team of muleteers (people who transport goods using pack animals, in this case mules). Mules are used for a whole host of transportation and logistics operations in Morocco, in our case to carry our overnight bags. In the Toubkal region, it is usual for each mule to have its own muleteer, whilst in other regions two or three mules may be looked after by one muleteer. The muleteers were much faster than our group and very skilfully guided their mules ahead of us so our kit would be waiting for us on arrival at our accommodation each night. These were the first muleteers I had ever met. It was a real privilege to be afforded yet another unique insight into a way of life so different from my own.

Leaving the valley floor we were soon surrounded by peaks, with some of the sun-exposed and lower slopes already bare and rocky, whilst the shaded areas and the high summits hung on to great depths of hard snow. Stopping at Sidi Chamarouch for lunch was a good opportunity to hear how the great boulder is a shrine, with the water emerging from beneath the rock said to have healing powers. As such, Sidi Chamarouch is a popular place of pilgrimage. After that, it was upwards to the Neltner Refuge, an Alpine-style hut with dormitory accommodation at an altitude of about 3,200 m. This was complete with the obligatory snorers and those who decided to sort out their kit at 11 p.m. with the aid of a headlamp which would have rivalled the Needles Lighthouse for brightness! Ear plugs definitely recommended.

Both our objectives were visible from here, with the refuge being situated at the very foot of Toubkal, whilst Ouanoukrim stood dominant at the head of the valley, accessible from a high col. Both looked stunning in their winter coats, if a little intimidating. Thankfully, our leader was very laid back, and had that inspiring calmness about him which I was recognising more and more amongst the leaders, guides and instructors I was now meeting. It was a calm presence, an authority, yet with a sparkle of fun in the eyes. I wanted to be like him!

Following a refresher of core winter skills on a snow slope just above the refuge, our group was all set. The following day, an early morning start allowed plenty of time for the obligatory slow-and-steady zig-zags which took us eventually to the high col at the head of the valley. It was an incredible spot, with views southwards towards the Sahara Desert seeming a little at odds with the hard snow beneath our crampon-clad boots. From the col an interesting bit of easy scrambling on rock and some steeper snow slopes led to the top. Our Ouanoukrim ascent was a success, giving me my first taste of a 4,000 m peak. I was so pleased, not just for the immediate achievement, but because of what else might be possible, building on this experience.

Unfortunately for our group, the weather the following day turned decidedly "Scottish" and our attempt on Toubkal had to be aborted from about the half-way point due to high winds and very poor visibility in the wind-blown snow.

It was still a wonderful trip though, and taught me an important lesson I would come to draw on frequently - turning back must always remain an option for a leader, regardless of how far the clients have travelled or how much money they have paid. Having cut my teeth in Scotland, I was well used to the idea that success, in terms of reaching a summit, is never guaranteed. In fact, success is about getting home safely; any summit is a bonus. Clichéd perhaps, but absolutely correct. Much later, in a professional capacity, I would often have to reach a sensible decision, and make that decision based on the grounds of safety alone. If the right decision is to turn back, it is still the right decision regardless of the fact that money may have changed hands and the clients may have travelled thousands of miles. Another really important skill of a leader is the ability to communicate the rationale for coming to such a decision, managing expectations in the face of poor conditions and finding the right balance between trying to achieve an objective whilst staying safe.

Such was the draw of Morocco that I booked a return trip as soon as I got home. When turning back without reaching a summit, it is often said that "the mountain isn't going anywhere". Toubkal certainly didn't go anywhere in the ensuing year, and it was fantastic to return in 2008 and make it to the summit (and back down!) safely. The group leader was even the same person as the previous year, so that made it all the more special for both of us.

MOROCCO - MULES AND MOUNTAINS

My first trip to Morocco was a fantastic experience and a great success, but what now? Climbing to over 4,000 m was fun, and I loved the whole experience of being abroad in the high mountains, living out of a trekking bag. What else could I do? Perhaps I could go to Nepal, a country I had always dreamt of visiting, but which had seemed a little out of my league. I had mentioned this possibility to our leader, who had led many trips to Nepal, climbing the likes of Mera Peak and Imja Tse (Island Peak) on several occasions. His response was, "You'd absolutely love it man, but you'll freeze your nuts!" What a sales pitch! It sounded like a plan.

Chapter 7

Decision Time

It is well documented that people returning from special trips can find it difficult to settle back into "normal life", whatever that might be. This seems to be particularly true of young people and is well known amongst those who go trekking and climbing in the greater ranges. Culture shock works both ways and is fully expected when travelling *to* an exciting and very different foreign destination. Yet after a period away, returning home can be surprisingly difficult. After the excitement of travel, the return to normal can seem mundane and your outlook on life will, almost certainly, have changed. "Folks back home", including good friends and family, may well find it very difficult to relate to tales of your travels. They may not be as enthralled by your stories and photos as you are, and may be envious that you've been away enjoying an adventure while they've been stuck at home. Parents will often hope their son or daughter will have "got it out of their system". The reality is very often just the opposite. Not to put too fine a point on it, returning home can feel very depressing after the initial thrill of seeing loved ones again.

There are no real shortcuts or remedies to avoid this problem, although certain things can help. From a practical point of view, it definitely helps to make sure you are not returning to an empty bank account. It helps if you have things to look forward to, and it may be possible to seek out a restaurant back home which will serve the local cuisine from your travels. (Although it has to be said, after a trip to Bolivia a few years later, I struggled to find a restaurant serving *cuy* [guinea pig] in Scotland!) Adventurous travels can also be brought back to life by regularly reviewing your photos and reading books about the country. This can be greatly enhanced by keeping a diary whilst you are away. However, the only real remedy is to start planning and saving for your next trip. You will not have "got it out of your system", much to your parents' dismay.

Back home in Stanley after Morocco certainly felt alarmingly ordinary. The usual post-holiday blues kicked in until I got back into the normal routine. One bonus was that after being up at 4,000 m, it turned out my bloodstream was packed full of red blood cells, so I was able to charge up and down some Munros with pleasingly little effort. I was feeling fit and ready for another challenge.

Soon enough I was back in the swing of my fishy scientific work, although my heart was still somewhere high amid the beauty of the Atlas Mountains.

My first post-doc was coming to an end as spring 2007 turned to summer. One of the big downsides of these academic research projects is that they are fixed-term contracts, typically lasting between one and three years, so it seems that no sooner have you settled into one than you are on the lookout for your next source of funding. However, I managed to apply successfully for my second post-doc position in the University of Aberdeen, this time working on a one-year project looking at the effects of temperature on reproduction in sandeels. I know, the excitement kept me awake at nights too! As had become usual for me, this was a joint project with the FRS, but this time with their Marine Laboratory in Aberdeen. The project went well and I was soon in the swing of my new surroundings, living in Aberdeen and enjoying the research and writing whilst continuing to explore the hills at every opportunity.

Aberdeen proved to be an interesting and at times fun place to live. The "Granite City" is so called because many of the city's buildings incorporate locally quarried grey granite into their construction. This can sparkle with a silvery appearance on sunny days due to its high mica content. Sadly, my project was only one-year long so I never got to see that. On overcast, rainy days, it could appear very bleak indeed. Aberdeen is a large city by Scottish standards, being the country's third most populous city, with an estimated population just shy of 200,000 people in the middle of 2012, yet relatively small in a UK context. Most famous as the oil capital of Europe since the discovery of North Sea oil in the 1970s, Aberdeen has flourished on the profits from this lucrative industry. Situated on the northeast coast of Scotland, Aberdeen is never going to win any warmth awards, yet it is a pleasant city with some lovely coastline nearby. I made the most of living in a city again by taking advantage of the theatre and enjoying regular five-a-side football. Importantly, it was also handy for the hills.

Living in Aberdeen I became even more familiar with the hills of Deeside, Lochnagar and the southern Cairngorms, and I always have a special affinity for these hills, partly because it's such a beautiful area, but also because they were some of the first areas I explored in Scotland. By now, I had also registered for my Summer Mountain Leader (Summer ML) - the benchmark hill walking award for taking groups out in the mountains, hills and moorlands of the UK and Ireland in summer conditions. I thought it would be good to try and consolidate my skills, but in truth, I had little idea of what the required standard was as I generally went out on my own. Still, I had a logbook now, so I started to record my trips to the mountains.

DECISION TIME

Having attended a couple of courses with Glenmore Lodge, Scotland's National Outdoor Training Centre, based near Aviemore, I was now on their mailing list. It was a pretty ordinary day in October 2007 when I got home from work and found their 2008 brochure lying on the mat. Flicking through it casually as I cooked my tea that night, I stumbled across their *Nepal Mountain* trip, and was hooked instantly. Glenmore Lodge (or simply "the Lodge", as it is affectionately known) was established in 1948, so 2008 was going to be their 60th anniversary year. To mark this milestone, the Lodge planned to run some one-off special courses and events. The *Nepal Mountain* trip was going to take place in October 2008, a full year from that point, and would involve a trek and climb in the Everest region of Nepal, trekking towards Everest before attempting to summit a peak called Lobuche East at 6,119 m. Climbing to this altitude would be a whole different ball game to what I had achieved to date, having climbed to 4,000 m previously in Morocco - a relatively modest altitude by comparison. The height of the peak meant the trip would be three weeks long, to allow for an appropriate acclimatisation regime. It would also involve my first experience of roping up for moving safely on glaciated terrain. In short, this was the real deal!

A massive appeal of the trip was that it would be led by married couple, Phil and Pauline Sanderson. At that time, both worked at the Lodge, Phil as a mountaineering instructor and Pauline as the marketing manager, though I had yet to meet either of them. They had both previously spent a lot of time living and working in Nepal. In fact, they were a pretty famous couple. Pauline was part of the EverestMax Expedition, the first expedition to travel successfully from the lowest point on land, the Dead Sea, to the highest point, the summit of Everest, by unpowered means. Phil had joined Pauline for the climb of Everest, making them the first British couple to summit the world's highest mountain at 8,849 m. Pauline's book *The World's Longest Climb* is certainly an inspiring read.

This was a chance to visit Nepal, a country I had dreamt of visiting for so long, and a one-off opportunity to go there as a student with the Lodge to attempt a 6,000 m peak. Wow! How do I get a place on this?!

I had decided this sounded like fun a long time before my tea was cooked that night. The key thing now was to secure a place on the trip. Thankfully, this didn't take long. The office at the Lodge was happy to take a provisional booking but, understandably, on the condition that I had a chat with Phil or Pauline to check whether my prior experience was suitable.

I was sat in my office in Aberdeen one day and the phone rang. It was Phil. His manner instantly filled me with confidence and, in my usual way, I probably underplayed my level of experience in the mountains. However, although I was pretty hill fit, I did want to impress upon Phil that I wasn't really a climber, but I had done a bit of scrambling and winter hill walking, as well as going to over 4,000 m in Morocco. Phil seemed perfectly happy and reassured me that not being a climber wouldn't be a problem. When I put the phone down the reality suddenly dawned on me. I was off to the Himalayas! At least I had a year to prepare. It's a young person's mistake; to fall into the trap of wishing your life away, looking forward to something that's happening a long way in the future.

* * * * * *

DECISION TIME

My second post-doc was drawing to a close as spring turned into summer 2008. Yet again it was time to consider my next source of employment. The usual trolling around for post-docs was revealing little that I could realistically apply for, and it looked like my scientific career was going to falter before it had really got going. It is a curious thing that getting a PhD may be viewed as the pinnacle of academic achievement among the general public, yet in reality, all it does is put you at the bottom of a long ladder, that ladder being the world of research. The PhD is just a minimum entry requirement, that's all. Nonetheless, it is still a great achievement and one of which I am proud.

Fortunately for me, an established and well-respected researcher at one of the Swedish universities had heard about me from one of my PhD supervisors, and invited me over, all expenses paid, to give a talk to his research group and to see his laboratory. This opportunity was welcomed. Sweden is a beautiful country I have been fortunate enough to visit a couple of times. The trip went well and my talk was well received and, apart from missing my plane on the way home, everything was pointing towards success. This was confirmed a few days later when an email arrived offering me a fishy post-doc in Sweden. Fantastic!

There is a saying that any good thing you care to name in life can be a bit like buses - you don't see one for ages, then two come along at the same time. Job offers, girlfriends … OK, so maybe not girlfriends in my experience, but so it turned out with job offers that week. A couple of weeks previously, another job had arisen, this time at the FRS Freshwater Laboratory in Pitlochry, with which I had been associated for several years prior to moving to Aberdeen. I was fortunate to be selected for interview, and was offered the job. Two job offers in one week!

I now faced something of a dilemma. To carry on down the academic research route, the Swedish opportunity seemed the more sensible option. I figured that if I got established with post-doc number three, I could then perhaps try and secure longer-term future funding whilst continuing to build up my growing publication list. I might also learn Swedish. So far the only word I knew was "fisk" (fish) and I figured there was certainly room to expand my vocabulary! This would hopefully put me in a strong position to apply for a research fellowship or lectureship somewhere in the not too distant future. I was certainly keen to move on from brief contracts and uncertainty.

Alternatively, I could take the job with the FRS Freshwater Laboratory, a good post which, although not strictly research, was still scientific. This option had a number of good points, such as the fact it was a permanent post, and I would be part of an active research community with lots of interesting projects going on which I would undoubtedly get to work on. This opportunity would also take me back to an area I loved, and where I would be quite happy settling. I had also worked out that the Swedish opportunity would be so far from the mountains (over three hours of driving) that visits there would become less viable. After careful consideration, I chose the opportunity which allowed me to stay in Scotland, and to carry on exploring the country I love so much, and which I was now proud to call home. Learning Swedish would have to wait.

This was an important decision point for me and, regardless of anything which may have happened subsequently, I never see the point in wondering whether a decision was the right one or not. As intelligent human beings faced with a choice, I believe we all have the capacity to weigh up the pros and cons of any particular decision, come to a conclusion based on the evidence available at that time and run with it, hindsight being a wonderful thing, of course. I see little merit in looking back and thinking how the other route might have turned out. Another path would surely have had some advantages but at the end of the day we choose a path and have no way of knowing how any other route would have turned out.

I had chosen to stay in Scotland. I wanted to climb more mountains.

Chapter 8

Mortgage

I started my new job in Pitlochry in June 2008. In the spring leading up to this I was incredibly busy, just to make a change. I was finishing up my Aberdeen post-doc and also had to prepare for moving back down to the area where I had lived for several years previously.

One of the big appeals of my new post was the possibility that I would actually be able to settle somewhere, and not be on the lookout for the next source of funding in a few months. Also, as it was a permanent job, I decided to buy a property rather than carry on renting. In my working life so far, I had had no option but to rent. No mortgage provider was ever going to look at me all the time I was working on short-term contracts, as there was simply no guarantee I would be able to continue making payments, or would even be staying in the same place. I found it frustrating that monthly rent payments, particularly in Aberdeen with its oil-based wealth, were typically higher than what I might be paying monthly on a mortgage for the sort of small place I would be looking to buy. It also seemed a shame effectively to "chuck money down the drain", as I viewed renting, as ultimately I had nothing to show for it. At least when paying off a mortgage you feel there is a goal at the end of it, namely securing a roof over your head. So it was that I tottered off one day for an appointment with a lady called Fiona (not one of my sisters!) who worked for a well-known high-street mortgage provider.

As it happened, this turned out to be relatively simple. I had the job offer letter which proved what my new salary would be, and Fiona helpfully worked through a number of scenarios for me, based on different amounts I might be looking to borrow and according to how much deposit I had to put down. It was easy for her to work out a ceiling as to how much I could borrow as I was single and would just have the one income. Armed with a few different numbers, Fiona assured me I was free to make an offer on a place up to a value of X, so long as I let her know within one month of our meeting. Simple.

It was surprisingly easy to move back down to the area between Perth and Pitlochry as I knew it very well, having lived in Perth for three years and Stanley for two years, and making regular visits to Pitlochry and much of the surrounding area. It will come as no surprise that my mortgage ceiling was fairly modest, to say the least. However, this was actually an advantage. By the time I ruled out places I couldn't afford (which was most of them) and places which were too far from Pitlochry, I was left with just a handful to view.

One sunny spring day towards the end of my post-doc, I left Aberdeen on a scheduled day off and headed south. I had made appointments to view a handful of flats which were within budget and in the right sort of area. I looked at a couple of places in Aberfeldy, one in Bankfoot, and one in Birnam. These three villages were all lovely, in my opinion, and any of them would have worked from a location perspective. Birnam seemed the best though, as it had a train station, useful for getting to Pitlochry if the A9 was shut or snowbound. In the event, one of the flats in Aberfeldy was too small and the other was too big. I was beginning to feel like Goldilocks. The flat in Bankfoot was very cosy, and would have done comfortably, but it was eclipsed by the flat in Birnam, which I viewed last. It was apparent as soon as I walked through the door that it was what I was looking for. In Goldilocks terms, it was just right. It was a small one-bedroom flat which formed part of a block of four. The interior was smart and modern, having recently been refurbished before the seller met someone whom she was going to move in with. She therefore had a beautiful little flat, all done up nicely, and she wanted to sell quickly! It was comfortably within budget and on the market for a fixed price - another bonus, as I could offer there and then without having to worry about someone putting in a higher bid. (More usually in Scotland, property is offered for sale with an "offers over" asking price, and it is up to potential buyers to submit a sealed bid. The eventual sale price is therefore typically above the initial asking price, particularly if the property is especially desirable.) I was more than happy to relieve her of it, so we shook hands before I headed off for a weekend of hill walking on Deeside. A quick phone call to the mortgage provider and the toing and froing of solicitors' letters commenced.

My parents came up to Aberdeen and helped me move to Birnam. They loved the flat and were pleased, as most parents are, I think, that I now had a "proper job", as they saw it, although to quote Dr. Hannibal Lecter in *The Silence of the Lambs*, "Not anymore"! Birnam itself turned out to be a lovely spot to live. It is a small village about half way between Perth and Pitlochry, just across the River Tay from Dunkeld. Right on the edge of the Highlands, the area is very pretty, a popular tourist spot, and has lovely walking and biking opportunities right from the front door. Villages in Scotland seem to have retained their hearts and services/ facilities much more so than those in England and the communities of Birnam and Dunkeld were very active. Despite their small size, I had a number of shops within walking distance, a doctors' surgery, a garage, car mechanic and filling station, and a mainline railway station, as well as a good bus service, post offices, little cafés, an Indian restaurant and takeaway (which was just a bit too handy to stop at on the way home from Braemar!) and an arts and conference/community centre. It was ideal for me and, of course, getting to the mountains was easy.

Birnam also has interesting literary connections. The village is home to the Beatrix Potter Exhibition and Garden. Although Beatrix Potter is most often associated with the Lake District, she spent much time in Birnam, Dunkeld, and the surrounding area, and her family's summer breaks in Dalguise had a strong influence on her development as an artist and scientist. There is also the Birnam Oak, an iconic tree standing adjacent to the River Tay in Birnam, celebrated in Shakespeare's play *Macbeth*, or "The Scottish Play". The Birnam Oak, together with the Birnam Sycamore standing next to it, are believed to be the only surviving trees of a forest once covering the banks and hillsides of the River Tay, known in *Macbeth* as the famous Birnam Wood. The prophecy of the three witches came true when branches of trees from Birnam Wood were used to camouflage the army marching against Macbeth. It is thought that a visit to the area in 1599 by Shakespeare provided him with the inspiration for this part of the play.

It was lovely moving to Birnam, but financially I was crippled. I had left my Aberdeen post-doc a few weeks early in order to take up the Pitlochry job, so ended up with two months of my Aberdeen rent to pay during the first two months of my mortgage repayment. My trusty little

Nissan Micra which had so valiantly undertaken all those trips up and down the M6 had also died during my time in Aberdeen, and I had replaced it with a Ford KA, generously funded largely by one of my brothers-in-law. This situation was far from ideal, but I knew it would sort itself out once it was just the mortgage. I had calculated carefully what my monthly outgoings would be and, once the liability of the Aberdeen flat was gone, I would be OK. I had also taken on board the kindly advice from said brother-in-law, who hinted with his usual but well-intentioned subtlety of a rhino, that really I needed to get some savings behind me so I had something put aside for a rainy day. I suspect the sort of rainy day he had in mind was when my car needed replacing, or I ended up having to rent somewhere and pay a mortgage at the same time. I took this in and vowed to look a little further ahead in future. It was advice which would transpire to be more than useful to me later on.

With Nepal on the horizon, and paid for some time ago, I wanted to make sure I was as hill fit as possible ready for October. It was great to be back in a more central position in Birnam and the mountains of Scotland's west coast were once again within range of a day's driving from home. My hill time therefore took on a more structured approach. I mixed up long days in the Cairngorms, frequently walking up to 20 miles and climbing a couple of Munros, with equally challenging days on the west coast, aiming for at least 1,000 m of ascent per day. This contrast was just what was needed. The Cairngorms lend themselves to covering big distances in a day, perfect for endurance training, whilst the spikier ridges and mountains of the west coast, starting more or less from sea level, build up the legs for big vertical ascents and descents over relatively short distances.

My second trip to Morocco also helped, climbing to over 4,000 m again. I felt this tidied up some unfinished business there, and it did no harm to get a few extra red blood cells manufactured ready for later in the year.

I settled in to my new job nicely. The first summer was spent getting up to speed with various things and, as I suspected, there were opportunities to get involved in some of the scientific research projects, as well as fulfilling my own role. I spent the weekends in the hills and October drew closer. One weekend in August, Phil and Pauline had invited all those booked on the *Nepal Mountain* trip to visit the Lodge for a day, to meet each other and to run over several aspects of the trip. This proved to be a really fun and useful day. The other participants seemed an enthusiastic bunch so I was confident we would all get along just fine. It was useful to go through the detailed kit list and ask lots of questions. The slideshow was very inspiring, showing the incredible scenery we would soon be immersed in, before we were let loose in stores to borrow any technical kit we needed for the trip. Saying our goodbyes at the end of the day, it was odd but nevertheless massively exciting to think that the next time we saw each other would be in Kathmandu!

Before driving back down the road from the Lodge to Birnam, I stopped in the dining room for a quick cuppa. There I chatted with Ellen over our cups of tea, as she had clearly had the same idea before her own drive home, to Inverurie. It turned out she would also be travelling alone on the trip, and we were each pleased that we would not be the only single people there.

So there I was in the early autumn of 2008, about to head off to the Himalayas. I was approaching 28 years old. So far in life I had managed to accrue 10 GSCEs at grades A* and A, 5 A-levels at grades A to C, a First Class Honours degree, and a PhD. I also had two post-doctoral research contracts under my belt, and a rapidly-growing list of academic publications. I owned a flat (or at least the mortgage provider owned the flat in which I lived) and a car, and had made a good start at travelling the world. I had taken my early obsessions with fish and fishing and ended up working with anything which had fins and lived in water. Somewhat ironically, this was at the expense of my sea angling which had now ceased, albeit entirely unintentionally, as I spent so little time in the south of England. Could my promising young talent ever have resulted in my wearing an England blazer, I wonder?

I was now a couple of months into a stable job in the public sector, with a regular income, associated pension and other benefits. My post-docs had also enrolled me in a university pension scheme, so I was starting to collect pension funds like some people collect stamps. Many of these things are what the world dictates to us as desirable, and which we should strive for. Job? Tick! Home bought? Tick! Pension scheme? Two ticks! Qualifications? Several ticks! Yet, even though I was working in a field relating to one of my main interests - even ticking a box on society's "nice to have" checklist - was that all there was to achieve, I wondered? I was also still young and single. Life was about to change.

Chapter 9

Nepal

The weeks and days leading up to the *Nepal Mountain* trip were filled with a healthy mix of excitement and trepidation. I was definitely hill fit and if anything I eased up a bit before departing the UK as I didn't want to go and twist an ankle or something similar. Despite having a good assortment of hill kit and having borrowed some technical kit from the Lodge, I had still bought quite a bit of kit for the trip. Lots of packing and repacking took place, until my big yellow North Face duffel bag and my trusty red and black Lowe Alpine rucksack were ready for the off. I flew down to spend the night with my parents before the trip and they kindly drove me to Heathrow Airport the following day. Heathrow never seems quite as mad since Terminal 5 was built, which seems to spread the insanity out a little. Nonetheless, it was still a rude awakening after the tranquillity of Birnam and it was a relief to get on the plane for a seven-hour flight to Doha, followed by a further five-hour flight to Kathmandu.

I was no stranger to travelling but even so, Kathmandu was something else! In a way it felt strangely familiar, I guess because of reading so much about it. The hotel where the group was to meet was centrally placed and very handy for the Thamel District of Kathmandu - the crazy trekkers' part of the city with numerous trekking agencies and outdoor gear outlets vying for your attention. I had deliberately flown out to Nepal a couple of days early in order to get over the flight and generally settle in, as a culture shock was guaranteed. It was enjoyable having that time to catch up with myself, alternating my time between

71

exploring the city, chilling out in the hotel, doing a bit of last minute sorting and of course, eating. During my casual browsing in Thamel I came across an interesting-looking powder. It appeared to be legal at least, and was in fact an orange-flavoured water additive. I grabbed myself a bag as I knew we would be drinking lots of water to aid our acclimatisation and, as it turned out, I found it to be really tasty and very helpful. It had the effect of turning water into a weakly-flavoured orange drink, a bit like weak orange squash, which I found a lot more palatable than just plain water. As with any food or drink product, the tastier it is, the more likely you are to eat or drink it, which in this case was good news for successful acclimatisation. This was to prove really helpful for this trip and was something I would remember on future high-altitude trips. The flavour also masked the feint taste of iodine if that was your favoured method of water purification. Whilst in the mountains I used iodine water purification tablets, with the orange-flavoured powder added post-treatment, but also took advantage of opportunities to drink boiled water as and when it was available.

The other group members arrived in due course and before long we were having our first in-country meeting as a group, with Phil and Pauline at the helm. Some more repacking was required as we were given a smaller duffel bag in which to pack our overnight trekking kit. The big duffel bags we had brought with us would contain just our mountain stuff and we would not see these again for a couple of weeks. Our overnight trekking kit would be carried for us by porters each day, meaning we just carried a day sack. Outdoor people love faffing with kit, so any excuse for another sort out was welcomed all round!

Sorted and packed, we enjoyed a group dinner watching some traditional local dancers, before our departure from Kathmandu the following day.

The airport at Lukla needs little introduction. Generally considered to be the gateway to the Everest region, thousands of trekkers and climbers fly in and out during the spring and autumn seasons. From an aviation perspective, however, it's pretty full on! Perched on the side of a very steep hill, the approach gives pilots one chance to get it right. Flying without radar relies on clear weather, so when clouds bubble up - typically late in the day - flights cease until it clears. After taking off from Kathmandu, our flight had to land at an intermediate airstrip as Lukla was clouded in. A brief break in the weather allowed us in to Lukla later that day and, when we were safely back on terra firma, we all agreed that the most dangerous part of the trip was probably behind us, apart from the return journey of course, which we still had to look forward to. Tragically, just two days after our flight in to Lukla, there was a fatal plane crash there.

Trekking days in Nepal take life back to a very simple rhythm. From Lukla, our route took us up the valley of the Dudh Khosi, passing through numerous Sherpa villages, including the largest settlement on the route, Namche Bazaar. Staying in lodges or teahouses, we would wake early and eat a hearty breakfast before getting on the trail. The weather is generally better in the morning, before clouds tend to roll in during the afternoon, often clearing again at night. Blue skies and cooler temperatures during the morning made for pleasant walking and spectacular photo opportunities amid the awe-inspiring scenery. Lunch would be eaten somewhere on the trail, usually outside surrounded by the most incredible mountain scenery, before walking on in the afternoon to our next teahouse. Our super-fit trekking crew would have got there long before us and our overnight bags would be ready and waiting.

Just as in Morocco, eating and drinking was greatly encouraged. Countrywide, the staple diet in Nepal is *dalbat*, *dal* being lentils cooked as a watery soup and *bat* being boiled rice. This would typically be accompanied by *takaari* (vegetables) and perhaps some meat, although it is a largely vegetarian diet because meat becomes increasingly difficult to digest at higher altitudes. That said, the odd "yak sizzler" I enjoyed was particularly fine. Lots of potatoes are grown in the region, and these wholesome fresh offerings typically formed the basis for lunch, again supplemented with a range of other tasty foods. The local people in the teahouses, and those cooking for us whilst camping, did us proud, preparing beautiful food day after day.

To deal with the effects of altitude, we adopted all the usual advice. Our daily height gain would not be too great and often during a day's trek we would climb higher before descending to our next overnight stop. This "climb high, sleep low" is effective at tricking the body into thinking you are actually higher than you really are, so the body works harder to deal with it, just as I had experienced in Morocco for the first time. Regular rest days were factored in to our itinerary, so after a couple of days trekking we would have the benefit of spending two nights in the same place. Rest days were "active rest days", meaning we would take a short walk to gain a little further altitude, before dropping to spend the night in the same place. One such example of this was spending two nights at Pheriche, enjoying a stroll on our rest day up towards Chhukhung and gaining grandstand views of Imja Tse (Island Peak). We also drank a lot of water on a little-and-often basis.

The scenery was just phenomenally beautiful, with steep-sided lush, green valleys giving way to the great glaciated peaks of the region: peaks such as Everest, Lhotse, Nuptse and Ama Dablam among the most famous, with strong supporting acts from lesser-known but just as spectacular peaks including Thamserku, Kangtega, Taweche, Cholatse, Pumo Ri, and of course, Lobuche East, our ultimate objective. We first spied Lobuche East one starlit night from Pheriche, where we had arrived on a cloudy afternoon. That night the skies had cleared and one of our group members had popped out from the teahouse to have a look round. Beneath the star-filled sky was the unmistakeable profile of Lobuche East, looking like a rather improbable objective from this angle!

Heading up the Khumbu valley, we followed part of the world's highest glacier, the mighty Khumbu Glacier, originating from the Western Cwm high up on Everest itself. Our highest teahouse, at Gorak Shep, was at the lofty height of 5,200 m, higher than all of the European Alps, yet at the bottom of the valley. Our objective for the following day was to climb Kala Patthar (5,545 m), the classic viewpoint looking across the Khumbu Icefall to Everest. The plan was to start walking before dawn, hoping to see the sun rise behind Everest. We had been told, however, to look out of the window when our alarm went off and, if we couldn't see the stars, to go back to sleep. I loved this method of weather forecasting and thought how great it would be to apply the same method in Scotland. "No, the mountains are covered in cloud today, we'll not go out." You'd never go anywhere!

When the alarm went off the following morning, I did as I was told, looking gleefully out of the window to see what the weather was doing. In my semi-awake altitude-induced dopiness, I was initially upset to see, well, not much. However, it suddenly dawned on me that there was a thin layer of ice on the *inside* of the little glass window. Ah ha, that's better - scraping off the ice and awakening a little more, I could see it was a clear night. We were in business. After getting up, it was a surreal scene as we sat in the communal area of our teahouse at Gorak Shep that morning. It was well before dawn, freezing cold, and we sat in the dimness in our down jackets trying to force our porridge down. We had little appetite, we were cold, and we felt sick. Happy days.

Our team was a little depleted as several members had stayed lower down the valley to aid their acclimatisation. Always willing to have a go, and knowing that feeling a bit off colour was entirely to be expected, four of us set off across the flat ground adjacent to the teahouse before commencing a slow plod up the broad ridge heading towards the top of Kala Patthar. The vertical height gain of just over 300 m would usually have been nothing, not even close to the height gain from the main ski-centre car park to the top of spot height 1,141 m in the northern Cairngorms. However, at over 5,000 m, everything was different now.

As we made our way uphill, painfully slowly, I wasn't feeling too good at all. I had a headache and my fingers were cold. Ellen had turned round (she has more sense than me) and was headed back to the teahouse with Pauline. I plodded on with another member of our group and, strangely, we both began to feel better as we headed up. Maybe it was because we were climbing and starting to warm up just a touch. Maybe it was because it was getting lighter by now. Maybe we were just stubborn.

Finding myself now part of a pair, we formed a little partnership. Psychologically I found it easier if I was in front. Not by much, and it certainly wasn't a competition, but I just found that with no one in front of me I could focus on putting one foot in front of the other, and that really helped. It turned out my partner found having me in front helpful as he had something to aim for. This teamwork worked well and, slowly but surely, we inched our way to the top, to be greeted by an incredible sunrise from behind Everest. Pauline joined us shortly afterwards, having trotted back up after making sure Ellen was back down at the teahouse safely. The three of us enjoyed some wonderful moments on the top of Kala Patthar. Even with my massive gloves on, my hands had been too cold to turn off my headlamp when it got light, but I finally managed it now as some welcome warmth arrived.

Heading back down to the teahouse at Gorak Shep was much easier than climbing up in the morning. I was a little off my lunch, and Pauline seemed concerned. I had been pretty good with the altitude up until now, but being off my food was not a good sign, as anyone who knows me would recognise! Pauline was keen to make sure I had a decent dinner that night. The afternoon was spent largely traversing or losing height, which was great. Losing even just a little bit of height makes a big difference to how you feel and it all helps with acclimatisation. Dzonglha was our destination where we were to spend the next two nights. This was also to be our final teahouse before heading up to Lobuche East Base Camp, where we would be camping.

I ate well that night and was now feeling good, much to my relief. Several of our team were back with us too and spirits were high. The following day we took a walk up to the Cho La Glacier where we spent some time practising the technical skills we would need on the mountain, including a useful refresher of crampon and ice axe skills and learning how to rope together for glacial travel. Back in Dzonglha for a second night further helped with our acclimatisation, especially since we had been up above 5,000 m again for the glacier training day.

By this time we had been reunited with our mountain bags and made our way up to Lobuche East Base Camp the following day. At over 5,000 m, it was a beautiful spot next to a little lake below the slopes of our objective. Here was to be our home for the next three nights, with our tents arranged neatly in a row on the little sandy beach. That evening I wandered over to a huge rock and sat there, among some of the world's highest mountains, lost in my own thoughts as the sun went down behind me. At this height, I was above the clouds which had done their customary job of filling in the valleys at my feet and, as darkness filled the valleys below, the last rays of the sun turned the white peaks first orange, then pink. Darkness eventually claimed the entire scene and thousands of stars came out to illuminate the black sky. Looking up, I soon recognised the unmistakable shape of Orion's Belt and I was immediately transported back in time, fishing on the shingle bank in the dead of night. Despite being years ago and thousands of miles away, it was as if I was standing on the beach with my father, watching the rod tip rattling away to the rhythm of the biting pout on this cold October night.

I suddenly remembered where I was and smiled to myself. I was so happy - happy to be here in the mountains, happy that I was feeling so good, happy that we had made it unscathed as far as Lobuche East Base Camp, happy that I was getting on so well with everyone in the group, especially Ellen - just so happy.

I was glad to have a bit of time to myself, despite how lovely the group was. A shared love of the mountains was making me realise that I was perhaps more of a "people person" than I had ever realised. I also knew I was at a turning point in my life. Despite my academic success and my current good job in science, it was the mountains which were inspiring me now. I realised that I was finding fulfilment in the mountains in a way I had never experienced before and not just here in the Himalayas, but back home in Scotland too. I had turned my hobby and passion into my career once already, in truth to their ultimate detriment. Was it foolish to think I could, or should, do it again? Sitting on a rock at Lobuche East Base Camp that evening, I realised I had changed. Other things now needed to change too.

By now it was very cold, so I returned to the tent I was sharing with Ellen. My down sleeping bag was very welcome and I lost myself in it, happy and contented. It would soon be time for dinner then bed, and I was looking forward to tomorrow.

At this altitude, it was well below freezing at night, so it was important to be aware of this and take some precautions, not only to look after ourselves but also our kit. It was customary to boil water before retiring for the night so we would have water available for drinking during the night and it gave us a "head start" for our drinking water the following day. A water bottle left unprotected inside the tent would freeze solid very quickly, so it was necessary to wrap something around it, perhaps a clean pair of socks. However, clean socks were something of a rarity, so keeping the water bottle inside my cosy down sleeping bag worked really well, protecting it from the cold air. I also made good use of lithium batteries in my camera and headlamp. Such batteries perform far better than any others in cold temperatures and similarly, I elected to keep these warm within my sleeping bag. It's a good job I'm slim as there was barely room for me!

Another consideration was that with all this water being consumed, it was necessary to pee frequently. In fact, such is the importance of drinking plenty of fluids to aid acclimatisation, there is a saying that "a good mountaineer always pees clear". That should perhaps be "an acclimatised mountaineer always pees clear". Whatever the saying, clear and copious was the aim. Perhaps rather oddly, I found the sight of clear pee immensely satisfying as it was an indicator I was acclimatising well. This was accompanied by a distinct lack of a headache and a general feeling of all being right with the world. Pee the colour of creosote, accompanied by a headache, is not a good sign at altitude. With all this clear pee about, a designated pee bottle is a strongly recommended piece of kit, allowing you to relieve yourself in the middle of the night without venturing from your tent into the freezing night. It is, however, important either to wrap a piece of duct tape around it, or have a different colour pee bottle from your water bottle ... In a dark tent in the middle of a Himalayan night, a water bottle and a pee bottle feel distinctly similar!

And while we're on this subject, another physiological effect of high altitude is a phenomenon known as High

Altitude Flatus Expulsion (HAFE). Probably self-explanatory, but for the sake of completeness, here goes! With increasing altitude comes decreasing air pressure. This causes a greater than normal difference in pressure between the gases inside the body and the outside air pressure, hence a greater urge to expel gas to relieve the pressure. It certainly brings a whole new meaning to the phrase "listening to the dawn chorus".

The following day continued the theme of acclimatisation, reconnaissance and practice. Some of our team headed up onto the lower slopes of Lobuche East to work out the best route for the morning, when we would be starting in the dark. We had a discussion about who was going to attempt the mountain and it was decided it would be Phil and Pauline with me and one other member of our group. The beauty of this sort of trip is that attempting the summit really is a bonus, and the trek and all other aspects of the trip can be achieved and enjoyed by many more people, even if they have no particular desire to summit a peak. That night we were certainly nervous, but with bags packed and dinner eaten, it was off to the sleeping bags for an early night and a pre-dawn start.

The night before a big climb is all about resting, not necessarily sleeping. However, just like a restless night at home when you know you have to get up early and it seems like you've had no sleep, it still comes as a shock when the alarm goes off. Traditionally, climbing on glaciated terrain takes advantage of an "Alpine start", a pre-dawn start at perhaps 3 or 4 a.m. This means climbing in the dark, taking advantage of the freezing conditions when the snowpack is frozen solid and at its safest, returning before the heat of the afternoon sun begins to destabilise the snowpack. After another surreal breakfast, this time in the mess tent with headlamp and down jacket, harnesses were donned and packs shouldered. Upon leaving my tent for the final time, Ellen kissed me and said, "Make sure you do everything Phil tells you to." At that point I would quite happily have stayed in the tent, but Ellen would never have let me. She knew what today meant to me.

Climbing in the dark was initially awkward, clambering up and over boulders and rubble with odd streaks of black ice, and I was glad when we got to the snowline. Here we stopped for Phil to rope us up. Continuing, we made slow but steady progress, moving together up the snow slopes towards the ridge above. The drill was for Phil to call "steady, steady", and we would move for 20 paces, then Phil would call "rest", and we would stop for a couple of moments to catch our breath amid the thin air of high altitude, before repeating. It might sound obvious, but essentially mountains are climbed by putting one foot in front of the other time after time, and this one was no different. Upwards we went until we got a brief respite as we reached the crest of the ridge. We stopped here for some drink and snacks, and I surveyed the scene. It was now light, and we could see where the last few hours of hard work had put us. For the past couple of weeks we had got used to wandering around with our necks craned back, gazing up at the most beautiful snow-capped peaks we had ever seen. Suddenly, we no longer needed to look up - we were level with them, on them, and there was no need to crane our necks. It was simply beautiful.

The ridge itself proved a worthy challenge, with Phil opting to pitch most of it. (Pitching means splitting the climb into sections or pitches between belays. A belay is the anchor system by which the rope, with attached climbers, is secured to the mountain.) This worked well as, apart from being very safe, it meant we got to rest while Phil led each pitch and built the next belay. He then got a bit of a rest while we climbed, with him belaying us from above. (Belaying is the process of using the rope to protect climbers as they ascend or descend.) With an Alpine grade of PD (peu difficile - slightly difficult), the ridge was probably about Scottish grade II, but the setting, exposure and altitude made it feel much more serious. It was tough, and one of those circumstances when, even though we were climbing well and making good progress, I didn't dare imagine we would actually make it to the top. However, after several pitches, Phil pointed at the summit, now just 100 m above us. Comfortably ahead of our turn-around time, it suddenly dawned on me that this was really going to happen! A couple of pitches later and I began to run out of ridge above me. A few more whacks with the ice axe and a few more kicks with the crampons, I looked up and Phil reached out a gloved hand to shake mine warmly. "Welcome to 20,000 ft, James."

I stood up and was on top of Lobuche East in the Himalayas, my first 6,000 m peak. I could have cried it was so beautiful, and the magnitude of the achievement dawned on me slowly - all the preparation, the dedication and the commitment, had paid off. I gazed around in awe, trying to bottle the view and my feelings at that moment, so I would never forget them, ever.

The panoramic views from the top were mind-blowingly beautiful. There was not a breath of wind and the sky was the unbroken deep blue of high altitude. Everest appeared to be within touching distance, yet was well over 2,000 m higher than us.

With four of us on the small summit, it was snug to say the least. There were lots of photos, hugs and back slaps, before the age-old mountaineering adage that the summit is only half way sprang to mind. The descent was uneventful, if tiring, and by the time we got back to the snowline, I was very aware of just how exhausted I was. I had to concentrate fully just to make sure I didn't catch my crampon front points on the other crampon as I walked. Normally this is simply a case of keeping your knees a little further apart than usual, and is something taught routinely on winter skills courses. Instructors talk about "the John Wayne walk" or "imagine there's a football between your knees". However, right now, nothing was easy. "Uncle" Ang Sherpa, one of our trekking crew, had wandered up to meet us at the snowline, bearing gifts in the form of the biggest flask of *chiyaa* (tea) I had ever seen. It tasted wonderful, and gave us the boost we needed to cover the rocky terrain back down to camp.

Ellen hugged me warmly when I got back, despite the fact I stank. Back in our tent my outer layers came off and I got curled up in my sleeping bag. I was asleep instantly and Ellen kept an eye on me all afternoon (it was still only the back of lunchtime when we got down), waking me each time one of our wonderful trekking crew brought round soup, hot drinks or biscuits. Ellen woke me again so I could have dinner as usual that evening, before an early night and probably the best night's sleep I've ever had. If I was happy yesterday, today had been off the scale!

Early the next morning it was time to get up and strike camp. We enjoyed a very leisurely breakfast on the little sandy beach, enjoying the sunshine and gazing up at the steep snow slopes of Lobuche East behind us. Had I really been up there?! It was now downhill all the way, and over the next three days we made our way back out to Lukla for our flight back to Kathmandu. As we descended, breathing became easier, the colours of the landscape became greener again, and the trails we had struggled to walk up nearly three weeks previously passed amid a blissful sense of achievement. First showers for weeks were taken in Namche Bazaar and, on our final night in Lukla before flying out, we said goodbye to Phil and Pauline and most of our trekking crew. We told them all it had been a life-changing trip, but we needn't have - they had known it would be before we even left the UK.

Our final night in Kathmandu gave us a great opportunity to celebrate as a team with a lovely meal out. There was a bit of excitement on the way back to our hotel as some civil unrest had broken out. Luckily we were "locals" by now, and took it all in our stride.

It was a long couple of flights back home, although a bonus was that one of my sisters came to pick me up from Heathrow Airport, so I got to spend a night with her and her husband. Their cats sniffed my bags very curiously on entering their flat, and the speed with which they moved away suggested they didn't particularly like the smell of three-week-old trekking socks. I was glad I had not used these socks to wrap my water bottle in.

Physically and mentally I was drained. I had not been ill at all, aside from a few very minor altitude-related symptoms during the middle of the trip. In fact, I had impressed myself with how well I had coped with everything. It had been tough though and, even without being ill, I had lost three quarters of a stone in weight, which took me nine months to replenish. I did have lots of red blood cells again though, so Munro bagging felt very easy for a while.

The big bonus of the trip, and something I had never even thought about beforehand, was that Ellen and I had got together, and she had kindly invited me to her place in Inverurie on the following weekend when we would both be home. There has been no mention of any romantic interest in my story so far, not for want of trying on my part. However, the few girls I had shown any interest in had not come to anything, and I probably had myself to blame, being a bit shy, moving around all over the place, and always being too busy fishing, or working, or writing a paper. Ellen had shown herself to be a thoroughly caring and loving person during our time together in Nepal, and we had shared an incredible adventure where everything had been so completely different to "normal life". As previously mentioned, returning home was likely to be a surprisingly difficult transition to make as such experiences can, albeit unintentionally, alienate you from those around you.

Meeting Ellen, after a largely solitary adult life so far, was a wonderful bonus and would ensure that going to Nepal was truly a life-changing experience in more ways than one. I was determined not to make a mess of things with her, but I was nervous about next weekend.

Chapter 10

Flowers And Chocolates

The return to normality after Nepal was tough. The inevitable pile of post waiting for me at home contained such exciting things as a gas bill. There were a few things to brighten the transition back to normality though. My parents had driven up to Birnam for the final week of my trip, partly so my flat wasn't empty for nearly a month, partly so there would be someone there when I got home and partly so they could enjoy some time in that beautiful area. It was lovely to see them. My first day back at work wasn't as bad as I had thought it would be either. It was late October and we had the first dusting of the new season's snow to low levels that morning. Everyone in work was glad to see me home safely, and they were intrigued with my tales. So much so in fact, that by popular demand, I put on a talk and photo show one lunchtime, which went down very well. Pleasingly, I also heard from Ellen who had by now got home to Inverurie safely, and was also finding the return to normality tough.

After my first week back at work, on Friday evening I headed up the road to Inverurie, located about 15 miles northwest of Aberdeen. I knew the way to Aberdeen well, but had never been to Inverurie. Ellen's directions were, in my humble opinion, somewhat ambiguous, albeit this was not clear until I was within striking distance. Anyone who has driven west from Aberdeen along the A96, past the airport and onwards in the direction of Inverness, will know there are many roundabouts between Aberdeen and Inverurie. Ellen's directions stated confidently that I should take the second roundabout after the airport. It quickly became apparent to me in my little Ford KA that this could not possibly be the case, with the second roundabout after the airport still being several miles from Inverurie. So I carried on. What Ellen meant was that I should turn off the A96 at the second of the *Inverurie* roundabouts. Silly me. Still, I told myself, perhaps this was a test to see how keen I was, a general initiative test, or simply a navigation test, albeit one which would rival any on a Winter Mountain Leader (Winter ML) assessment.

Ellen was delighted to see me, suggesting I had passed the initiative and navigation tests. Ellen was further impressed by the fact that I was wearing a shirt as opposed to a base layer, and I had even had a shave. Still, before knowing these things, it was a nervous man who seemingly attempted to hide behind the bunch of flowers and box of chocolates he had bought, as the door was opened and a welcoming embrace ensued.

Ellen had prepared a beautiful three-course dinner for me and, as anyone who knows me will testify, it's fair to say I appreciate my food! However, having got through the initial tests unscathed, it dawned on me that I should probably return the favour next weekend and invite Ellen down to Birnam. But how on Earth was I going to compete in the culinary department?! My invitation was accepted graciously, which gave me the best part of a week to dream something up. Having survived on what Ellen might charitably describe as "student food" until the ripe old age of nearly 28, it looked like I was going to have to up my game. In truth, if I'd had a year to dream something up, I probably wouldn't have done any better. Still, Ellen arrived in Birnam on the following Friday evening, and appeared to appreciate my "mince and tatties" concoction.

FLOWERS AND CHOCOLATES

My appreciation for Ellen's food was further highlighted some time later. It was the middle of winter and I had been up at Ellen's for the weekend. Come Sunday afternoon Ellen had kindly made me stew and a bowl of homemade soup for lunch before I drove back down to Birnam. She had also popped a plastic tub containing another portion of stew in the car for me, so I would have something quick and warming to eat when I got home, along with a portion of soup. Later that evening we were chatting on the phone and I thanked her profusely for the stew and soup.

"You didn't eat all that, did you?!" It wasn't really a question.

"Yes, the soup was lovely, and the stew was great too. I had them with some bread and butter."

"You fat pig," came the response. "That soup was meant for you to take in to work on Monday."

"Oh dear," I replied. "Well they were lovely, and if I bring back the empty tubs next week, can I get a refill please?" It was worth a try.

We both found it tough to adjust back to normality after Nepal. Even putting our new-found relationship aside, we had both found the Nepalese experience to be truly life-changing. Our view of the world had been tested greatly, meeting and mixing daily with the locals, people who have very few material possessions by western standards, yet who were some of the happiest and most enterprising people you could ever have the pleasure to meet. We think of ourselves in the west as doing well to recycle a few envelopes and glass bottles, yet the people of Nepal will build a house out of seemingly nothing, recycling materials gleaned from elsewhere. Oh, and they do it all with hand tools, on the side of an impossibly-angled slope.

I also think it is fair to say that we were both a little apprehensive about whether we could make a "holiday romance" work. Clearly we had shared a wonderful trip together, and had plenty of things to talk about initially, yet would we be compatible long term? As it happened, our relationship flourished. We were both fiercely independent, having each lived alone and done exactly what we wanted for so long, with very little need to consider anyone else, and this would inevitably take some adapting by us both. Ellen loved cycling and I loved climbing mountains. We had got together in a country which was half way around the world, and it turned out we lived just two hours apart from one another. Most importantly, we were happy together.

Above left: Old habits die hard - tiddler fishing in a New Forest stream during recent years. © Ellen Thornell, 2013.

Above right: A proud day - graduating with my PhD from Cardiff University. © Tony Orpwood, 2006.

Below: My first wreck fishing trip - an 11 ½ lb. pollock caught aboard Sundance II. A similar photo appeared in the *Southern Daily Echo*. © Roger Bayzand, 1995.

Above: A busy night in the Djemaa el Fna, the famous square in Marrakech, Morocco. Note the smoke coming from the food stalls. Photo by the author.

Below: Toubkal (4,167 m), North Africa's highest mountain, taken from high up on Ouanoukrim (4,088 m), Morocco. Photo by the author.

Above: On top of Lobuche East (6,119 m), Nepal.
© Pauline Sanderson, 2008.

Below: Lobuche East Base Camp, Nepal. Photo by the author.

Above: Llamas grazing, Bolivian Andes. Photo by the author.

Left: Pequeño Alpamayo (5,370 m), Bolivia. Note the pair of climbers, bottom left. Photo by the author.

Above: Hrútsfjallstindar (1,875 m), Iceland - a beautiful peak on the edge of Europe's largest icecap. Photo by the author.

Below: Early morning reflections at the start of a big day climbing Hrútsfjallstindar (1,875 m), Iceland. Photo by the author.

Above: Rock climbing at Pinnacle Crag, Duntelchaig.
© Ellen Thornell, 2018.

Left: Trying my best to keep up with Ellen - heading up Glen Einich, Cairngorms. Photo by the author.

Right: The freedom to enjoy responsible wild camping in Scotland is a great privilege. © Ellen Thornell, 2009.

Above: Enjoying classic Lake District scenery - looking down from High Stile towards Crummock Water and Bleaberry Tarn. Photo by the author.

Below: The author checking the map between Wandope and Crag Hill, the Lake District. © Ellen Thornell, 2018.

Above: With the Cairngorms in the grip of winter, a walker makes her way towards the summit of Meall a' Bhuachaille. Photo by the author.

Below: Looking towards Braeriach from near the summit of Sgor Gaoith, Cairngorms. Photo by the author.

Above: Nestling in the heart of the Cairngorms, Loch Etchachan is a very special place. Photo by the author.

Below: It all started with a trip to Nepal! Ellen and I on our wedding day.
© Sandy Fea Photography, Inverness, 2011.

Above: A true honour - leading former world shore angling champion, Chris Clark, on his charity hike up Ben Nevis. Chris holds the British Citizen Award for Service to Education (BCAe) in recognition of his dedication to coaching young talent. Photo by the author.

Below: A classic route up Ben Nevis - the Carn Mor Dearg (CMD) Arête. Photo by the author.

Chapter 11

Summer ML

With 2009 upon us, life had settled into a new normal. Ellen and I loved spending the weekends together, either in Inverurie or in Birnam, from where we went off hill walking, cycling, or just enjoying a low-level wander and each other's company. We reminisced frequently about those wonderful weeks we had spent together in Nepal and I enjoyed working hard to replenish the three quarters of a stone in weight I had lost. It was tough, but I managed it eventually.

I used nearly all of my leave allocation from work during that year to undertake training courses in mountain activities. One of the most memorable courses occurred at that magical end of March/early April period, when the weather in Scotland generally improves considerably, and I went on a winter scrambling/mountaineering course on the west coast. The ratio for this course was meant to be up to four students with one instructor. However, in the event it was just me and one other student with our instructor. Given the low student-to-instructor ratio, and given that the pre-course chat revealed the other student and I both had a good deal of experience, the instructor declared confidently that the two of us would be bored if we stuck to the syllabus, so we would ditch it and just go and have a great big adventure on the west coast! It's important to note here that on such skills courses, the syllabus is a guideline only, and can, to an extent, be tailored according to the students' prior experience and aspirations. Certainly there is more flexibility than when undertaking a National Governing Body qualification training course, such as the Summer ML or Winter ML schemes, for example. This attitude of being flexible with plans and adapting to a client's needs was an important lesson and something I made a mental note of for the future.

We definitely got our money's worth on this course! With a developing high pressure system through the week, the last three days were spent on the Aonach Eagach in Glen Coe on Wednesday, on Tower Ridge, Ben Nevis on Thursday, rounding things off with Curved Ridge, Buachaille Etive Mor, on Friday. These are absolute classic Scottish mountaineering days, among the best I have ever experienced in the British mountains.

Returning to base on the Friday evening, Ellen was waiting for me. My grin gave the game away before either of us spoke, it rivalling the one I had had on my face many years previously when I caught those two big cod on an October boat trip. Ellen looked suspiciously at the pair of climbing axes I was about to return to stores.

"What were they for?" she said.

"Well," I said, "It was a great week of weather and there were only two of us on the course, so we were able to do a bit more. We needed the climbing axes for our day on Tower Ridge on Thursday. It's grade IV in winter."

"Oh I see," said Ellen. "I thought you were going on a winter scrambling course."

I was keen to undertake courses such as this for a few reasons. First and foremost, this course and others like it were fun. Let's be honest, why would you bother going to all the effort of climbing mountains if you didn't find it fun, even if that's type II fun? (Remember, that's when it's fun back in the safety of the warm bar at the end of the day.) Such courses were also important for my personal development, as I was learning a lot of new skills and getting the opportunity to practise them in context under the watchful eye of an instructor. Additionally, such courses meant I was able to do things which were well above the technical level of what I would be able to achieve safely under my own steam. Climbing Tower Ridge in winter conditions as part of a course was a case in point - a phenomenal experience and certainly way above anything I could have led personally at the time. The Aonach Eagach and Curved Ridge weren't bad either!

However, another reason for undertaking training courses was that by now I was certain the outdoors was where I wanted to work. I had been inspired massively by my experiences in Morocco and Nepal, and loved everything about the Scottish mountains back home. I had made a very definitive decision to stay in Scotland at the expense of pursuing my earlier academic career. I was also in awe of the outdoor professionals I was now meeting on a regular basis, many of whom were at the top of their game. Yet, rather than see their tremendous achievements as intimidating, it inspired me further. I was well used to mixing with the best in the business. During my sea angling days I had fished alongside, and, more importantly, learnt from, one of the top charter fishing boat skippers in Britain, a former world shore angling champion and several regulars in the various England teams. I had also had the privilege of working alongside some world-class academics and scientists. I could mix with the best.

Luckily, Ellen knew from the outset that I was looking to change direction in my professional life, and was incredibly supportive from the word go. We knew it would take time to engineer a complete change of career and lifestyle, and I knew I wasn't going to get paid to go hill walking - life could never be that good, could it?! However, the reality was at that point I had no idea about the outdoor industry, how broad it was, or how to get into it. What I did know though, was I loved being outside, in the mountains, on a mountain bike, or just pottering around. It didn't really matter. I also knew there were plenty of people making a living from the outdoors, and I also knew I needed to get some qualifications, so that seemed like a good place to start.

It had now been a couple of years since I first registered for my Summer ML. In contrast to when I had first registered, however, I now had definite aspirations to obtain the award for professional use. Many people will undertake this award for purely personal reasons. To pass it demonstrates a high standard of competency, even if you have no intention of using the award in a professional context. Nonetheless, from a professional perspective, this award opens up a lot of work opportunities in its own right, and is also a pre-requisite award which must be obtained before undertaking either the Winter ML or Mountaineering and Climbing Instructor (MCI) schemes. As such, the Summer ML is an essential qualification.

Most people take several years to complete their Summer ML, a process involving personal experience, a formal training course, a consolidation period, and a five-day assessment. I was no different, having only started in earnest in 2003, and it was now six years later. This is not a process you will get through by accident, and it takes a great deal of time and dedication to complete. There are pre-requisite elements in order to proceed through to assessment, including leading groups, and this element is often achieved by candidates taking out family, friends and other willing "guinea pigs". There is also a minimum number of nights' wild camping which must be completed prior to assessment.

In truth, I had stacks of experience in the mountains in summer, and having chatted with Phil and Pauline at length in Nepal, they assured me I was ready for the training course. Or to put it another way, Pauline gave me a proverbial kick up the arse to get on with it. The instructor on that fabulous course on the west coast also knew of my aspirations and proved to be an encouraging and inspiring influence throughout, long after the completion of the course.

So it was that in May 2009 I attended the six-day Summer ML training course. Such was the success of this week that I went home and booked my assessment for October the same year. There is nothing like having a target date for making something happen and, when it boiled down to it, all I really needed was to get my required nights of wild camping in the mountains, get my emergency rope work slick, and practise, practise, practise my navigation. That wasn't much if I said it quickly. What could possibly go wrong?

The freedom to enjoy wild camping in Scotland is a great privilege, and should be exactly that - wild. This type of camping is lightweight, done in small numbers and only for two or three nights in any one place. Importantly, it should be carried out away from farms and farmland, buildings, roads or historic structures. It should follow the principles of "leave no trace" whilst also considering other important access considerations, such as those around deer stalking and grouse shooting. Putting up a tent at the back of a car park is not wild camping!

A common theme was developing with my journey into the outdoors, and that was the gleeful acquisition of more kit. This was akin to my purchasing an ever-increasing number of fishing rods in years gone by, because another was always needed for one very specific set of circumstances. After my Summer ML training course, when I had shared a tent with another participant, Ellen and I wasted no time in purchasing a decent tent and stove. The tent choice was important - we wanted it to be big enough that we could use it when we were out together, but light enough so I could carry it when I was out on my own. We eventually found what we were looking for, and were not disappointed. It was plenty big enough for us both, felt like a spacious palace when I was alone, yet weighed very little. We joked about it being the first "home" we had bought together, thus a meaningful step forward in the relationship. If we eventually went our separate ways, who would gain custody of the tent?! I suppose we could have cut it in half.

Ellen and I love wild camping, but we were both very aware that the immediate priority was for me to get slick with a view to the assessment and beyond. At least, that was Ellen's excuse for having increasingly little to do with the process of putting the tent up and getting water on to boil for a welcome hot drink! She was right, of course and, as the number of trips we did increased through that summer, Ellen took more and more of a back seat so I could get into a natural routine of arriving at the overnight spot, locating a suitable site, pitching the tent, getting the kit in the dry and getting a brew on. We could then sort sleeping kit and get some dinner on the go, safe in the knowledge that we were where we needed to be, our kit was in the dry, and we were warm, fed and watered. This is important for a leader as it demonstrates a "lead by example" approach, besides which it is important for the leader to look after their personal well-being. If they do not, they will not function as effectively in their leadership role.

In the early days of our wild camping exploits, we also had a little helper called Hug Me. Hug Me was a small fluffy bear which I had "rescued" from a shelf in the departure lounge of Cardiff Airport and given to Ellen as a gift. He accompanied us on a few wild camping trips before being retired due to the trauma he sadly experienced. On one occasion in Glen Derry, he managed to fall out of Ellen's pocket when she went to fill our water bottles from the stream. It turned out Hug Me is not very good at back stroke, but he does float, and so was successfully retrieved to dry out. Another traumatic experience, this time for both Hug Me and Ellen, occurred one night near Ben Lawers. We had pitched our tent and enjoyed dinner, and the plan was that I would head out for some night navigation practice before going to bed. Ellen, ever the sensible one, remained in the tent to read a book. I duly tottered off, with no particular plan in mind, and eventually wandered up to the top of Meall nan Tarmachan, a pleasant Munro near Loch Tay with fabulous views, particularly to the west. Here I sat, waiting for it to get dark. The sun eventually set as a bright orange ball, sinking behind a great bank of cloud which had appeared from nowhere in the far west. I waited a little longer (it takes a long time for it to get dark in Scotland in the summer; no quick Caribbean-style sunsets here!) before putting on my headlamp and heading back to the tent, avoiding the path in the main to practise some contour interpretation, map and compass skills at night. Unluckily for Ellen, I found the tent first time, by now long concealed by the darkness. Ellen graciously unzipped the door to the tent and grudgingly allowed me in, complete with an enormous halo of midges flying around my head and headlamp! We hastily zipped the tent door back up and did our best to squash the not inconsiderable number of midges which had snuck in to the tent with me. Domestic bliss continued the following morning when we took Hug Me out of the little pocket on the inside of the tent where he "slept". The pocket was full of dead midges. Poor Hug Me.

Amazingly, Hug Me survived to fight another day, but now resides in a warm bungalow in Aviemore, having only to tolerate two humans who seem to pop in with amazing regularity.

Continuing the theme of wild camping and navigation practice during my consolidation period, Ellen and I frequented the Cairngorms with pleasing regularity, often with our sights set on the area around Ben Macdui. I love it up there - the highest point in the middle of what is generally referred to as the Cairngorm Plateau, and the second highest mountain in the UK. Indeed, before the production of accurate maps, it was debated whether Ben Macdui was in fact higher than Ben Nevis. However, following surveys of both peaks in the period 1846 to 1847, it was confirmed that Ben Nevis is higher, and is indeed the highest peak in the UK. There followed plans to erect a huge cairn on the top of Ben Macdui to make it higher! Those plans never succeeded.

Traditionally approached from either Speyside in the north or Deeside in the south, I would not have to think too long to come up with half a dozen routes, all culminating on the Arctic dome of Ben Macdui. Its height and position mean the weather can be extreme. There are days when there is not a breath of wind and no sound whatsoever, except the crunch of snow beneath your boots. Equally, there are days when visibility is reduced to that common Scottish phenomenon of "the white room", when complete snow and cloud cover combine to give nothing whatsoever for the eyes to focus on. Combined with heavy falling snow and a high wind, the Cairngorm Plateau respects no one.

A trig point is a fixed pillar, typically made of concrete, used in conjunction with other trig points for geographical surveying purposes using triangulation. They are found at the tops of many hills and mountains, including at the top of Ben Macdui. It is always something of a relief when, having crossed the plateau following nothing but your compass needle for the past three hours, the trig point appears from the gloom, even if that is more or less by bumping in to it. Such days do little to refute the idea of a presence or creature said to haunt the area, *Am Fear Liath Mòr* in Scottish Gaelic, the Big Grey Man.

On one trip, Ellen and I had wild camped at Derry Lodge, before proceeding up Glen Derry and heading up towards Loch Etchachan via the Hutchison Memorial Hut. Despite it being mid-summer, the weather was decidedly "iffy", with a damp blanket of cloud and drizzle coming and going. Sensible as ever, Ellen decided to wait at Loch Etchachan while I headed up to Ben Macdui before returning for a cup of tea. With the summit located safely, it took just a couple of compass bearings to get me back to the loch, Ellen, and the stove for the much-awaited brew. Strangely, just a week or so later, we were back in very similar circumstances, but this time, a rather soggy and bedraggled-looking Duke of

Edinburgh group was just returning from the summit as we reached the loch on our way up. Ellen, who isn't such a fan of Ben Macdui as I am, would not hear of waiting at the loch today. "If they can do it, so can I!", so off we went for another wetting and a bit more compass work.

These experiences were incredibly important to prepare me for my forthcoming assessment. We were able to look at different options for things such as food. For example, dehydrated camping meals are lighter to carry, but when you boil water to rehydrate them, that water is used to make the food, meaning you have to boil a second lot of water to have a soup or a hot drink. "Wet" camping meals are heavier to carry, but are effectively "boil in the bag", so once your food is ready, that same water can be used for a brew, thus saving gas. Aside from these quite focussed preparations, it was of course important to remember the very essence of why I was there - I love being in the mountains and I wanted to share that love with others. Meeting with Ellen on a Friday night at a random car park, heading in to the hills for the weekend, pitching up in a remote glen or high up on a slope with only the red deer for company - this was getting to feel more and more like normal life. We were happy about that.

The assessment was tough, as expected, being put through my paces during the five-day course. It seemed difficult to settle in to the first couple of days, ticking off parts of the syllabus such as river crossings, emergency procedures, security on steep ground, group management etc., but once out on the three-day, two-night expedition, I was away. This was the very essence of the activity for me - roaming around the Cairngorms with an expedition rucksack on my back, navigating around to climb some peaks and complete an interesting and varied route in the mountains whilst spending time with some engaging folk. During these assessments, the "group" that you lead is your fellow candidates. Each of you takes a turn at leading the group, taking them (hopefully!) to the spot dictated to you by your assessor, dealing with any and all appropriate group management issues as you go. Our expedition was actually very enjoyable and, despite the obvious pressure of being assessed, was a fabulous experience. There's nothing like being up on the Cairngorms at night, following your compass around, to give you the confidence to think, "Yes, I can do this."

It was an anxious time back at base at the end of the week, eating lunch and waiting to be called for my debriefing and result. But it was an immensely proud moment when my assessors shook me by the hand and congratulated me on passing my Summer ML. My certificate would arrive in the post in due course, but for now I was content with the warm fuzzy feeling of success, and the promise of a shower, a hot meal and somewhere to dry out all my kit in Inverurie, much to Ellen's delight. My journey towards becoming an outdoor professional had really begun.

Chapter 12

Special People, Special Places

Completing my Summer ML successfully was certainly a significant point in my life, but it would be rude at this juncture not to mention another important milestone which also came to pass in 2009.

The Cairngorm Mountains are, in my humble opinion, magical, partly due to their grandeur and mystery. From a hill walking perspective, the three main massifs of the Cairngorms are traditionally approached from either Speyside in the north, or Deeside in the south. These massifs are the Braeriach/Cairn Toul group in the west (including the Glen Feshie hills), separated by the great gash of the Lairig Ghru from the Ben Macdui/Cairn Gorm group of the central Cairngorms. These in turn are separated by the Lairig an Laoigh from the hills of the eastern Cairngorms, notably the Beinn a' Bhuird/Ben Avon group.

Curiously, the name "Cairngorms" is something of a modern inaccuracy. The true name of the mountains in Scottish Gaelic is *Am Monadh Ruadh*, meaning the red rounded hills, reflecting the pink granite from which they are made. This distinguishes the Cairngorms from the mountains of the Monadhliath to the west of the River Spey, *Am Monadh Liath*, meaning the grey rounded hills. I find Scottish hill names fascinating, tending to be very descriptive, reflecting the fact they were named a long time before the Ordnance Survey, or indeed anybody else, was interested in their heights. One example of how mountains were named before anyone had measured their heights is well illustrated by two of the Lochaber giants near Fort William. Aonach Mor (meaning "big ridge") is actually lower in height than its nearby neighbour Aonach Beag (meaning "small ridge"). Their names refer to their relative bulk when seen from the glens, rather than their height above sea level. Perhaps people living in the glens during ancient times named Scottish hills for their purposes of "sign-posting" the landscape, enabling them to move themselves and their animals around, conduct trade and so on. Colours will frequently feature in hill names, as will words to describe their shape, so you can tell a lot about what a particular mountain might look like just from its name.

Five of Scotland's six highest mountains are located in the Cairngorms - Ben Macdui (1,309 m), Braeriach (1,296 m), Cairn Toul (1,291 m), Sgor an Lochain Uaine (1,258 m) and Cairn Gorm (1,245 m). Geologically, the Cairngorms are formed from rough weathered granite, forming high plateaux, sculpted by ice during the last ice age. Britain's only sub-Arctic landscape, numerous corries and deep, almost trench-like, glens bit deep in to these high plateaux. Home to a host of rare species, snow can lie for much of the year on some of the highest slopes sheltered from the sun, spots such as the northeastern flanks of Ben Macdui and the high deep recesses of Garbh Choire Mor on Braeriach. These mountains are vast, and it takes a while to grasp the scale of them; too big to be appreciated from below, the only way to experience their scale is from up high, and here the weather can be extreme.

I have no intention of entering into a debate about which other mountain groups may or may not be considered part of the Cairngorms. The majestic Lochnagar to the south of Deeside is generally considered to be part of the Cairngorms, and indeed, the establishment of the Cairngorms National Park in 2003 included large swathes of other hills within its boundaries, notably those to the south of Lochnagar (the Angus Glens and the hills of Glen Shee) and hills to the north of Blair Atholl. One thing is certain - you could spend a lifetime wandering these mountains and still find new places to explore.

Another thing was clear to me many years ago, and that is I would love eventually to live in Aviemore, in the northern Cairngorms. The area around Aviemore had always been very special to me. I also love the area around Braemar, in the southern Cairngorms, having got very familiar with the region when I first came to Scotland, and more so when I lived in Aberdeen. Among the delightful little village's numerous attributes, Braemar has a beautiful duck pond with some of the friendliest and most enthusiastic ducks I have ever encountered. Indeed, even Braemar's dubious claim to fame of having twice recorded the lowest-ever UK temperature of -27.2 °C (in February 1895 and January 1982) wouldn't have discouraged me from living there. The only thing which did put me off ever living in Braemar is that getting to the west coast, and indeed other areas of the Highlands in general, would be trickier from there. Aviemore, on the other hand, offers a very central location, is a pleasant place in its own right, and allows easy access to many other parts of the Highlands. It is also just a stone's throw from the likes of the northern corries of Cairn Gorm and the hills of Glen Feshie. Another major attraction is the plethora of beautiful low-level walking and cycling which can be enjoyed in the area, with beautiful areas of Caledonian Forest, rivers and lochs. It's not even too far from the coast. Yes, Aviemore would be home one day.

Thankfully, Ellen shared my enthusiasm for the area. It was apparent to both of us that the area was very special to us as a couple. We had met because of a trip organised through the Lodge. We knew quite a few folk in the area and it felt like home anyway. We hated leaving there whenever we went home, even though, to be fair, we each lived in a great location as it was.

On one particular Saturday in May 2009, we drove up from Birnam and went for a wander towards Loch Morlich from Glenmore, as we had done so many times before. This day was special though. It was hot and the sun was doing its best to burn a hole in Scotland. Something else was special too and when we stopped by the crystal-clear waters of the stream which runs in to Loch Morlich, I retrieved the little box which I had tried so hard to conceal from view. In it was a ring, and the answer was "Yes". Ellen and I were going to get married.

As with most things in life, timing is everything. Being an old-fashioned sort of person, a couple of weeks previously I had asked Ellen's father, John, for her hand in marriage. Telephoning him was perhaps not the most traditional means of communication, and I would have preferred to have spoken with him face-to-face. However, with us in Birnam/Inverurie and him down in Westerleigh, just outside Bristol, it was a pragmatic approach, and I am sure if I had flown down "just" to ask him that, he would have called me a bloody idiot.

It was a Saturday and I was going hill walking, just to make a change. I was on my own that weekend - I think Ellen was competing in a cycle race. It was going to be a very hot day and my plan was to climb the two Munros to the west of Loch Treig, the steep and shapely Stob a' Choire

Mheadhoin and Stob Coire Easain, linked by a high bealach (col). Such was the importance of the telephone call to my prospective father-in-law that I decided to drive to the small car park at Fersit first, and make the call from there, just in case making the phone call delayed me to the extent that there was nowhere to park when I arrived. I had no idea whether I would get a phone signal from Fersit, but I needed my hill fix and it was going to be a cracking day. Thankfully for me, I did get a signal, so I dutifully rang John and posed the question. I was extremely delighted and humbled when he agreed, albeit a little surprised when he also wished me luck. That's odd, I thought; I wonder what he meant by that?

Back to the issue of timing, Ellen's father was an inspiring man. Blind from his late 30s, he led a very active life and always showed great interest in people. He bred a long line of champion goats over forty or so years. On the day I chose to phone, however, one of these goats had just died. Oops! It was not the best timing on my part.

On an incredibly sad day towards the end of 2017, we laid Ellen's father to rest in Westerleigh, the village where he was born, where he had lived all his life, and where he died. RIP, John.

Chapter 13

Making Promises

It was to be another two years before Ellen and I got married. We were in no particular rush and were enjoying life. We both had decent jobs and were enjoying our time together. I was content, for the time being at least, to chip away at getting as much experience in the outdoors as I could, knowing my chances of successfully making a transition into the industry would be greatly helped by having a few qualifications under my belt. Having my Summer ML in the bag was a good start, but I had a long way to go.

Anyone who has ever planned a wedding will know that things can quickly spiral out of control. The basic idea of a wedding seems pretty simple, and the sentiment expressed by the character George in the film *Father of the Bride* will ring true. "Getting married" and "a wedding" are indeed entirely different! It is also the case that any normal product with the "w" word put in front if it instantly makes it cost triple what it probably should. Ellen and I were determined not to get sucked in by all of this, for several reasons. Firstly, we had seen it all before. Large expensive weddings costing a fortune are certainly no guarantee of future happiness or longevity of relationship - just ask the Royal Family. Secondly, we could not afford to spend a fortune on a wedding. We are strong believers that if you can't afford something you either go without or save up until you can afford it. Not particularly romantic maybe, but we saw little point in running up a massive debt for a few hours of enjoyment which we would end up paying for well into the future. Besides, no one was offering to pay for our wedding, and why should they? This was a decision we had made, we were both grown-up adults, each well established in a good job and with a property, and this was another lifestyle choice like any other. It would not be fair to expect anyone but us to fund something of our choosing.

Fortunately for us we didn't want a big wedding anyway. We both knew plenty of people through our respective jobs and Ellen's cycling, but decided to take the easy option of restricting the guest list to just immediate family and a couple of very close friends. This would save any embarrassing moments, we thought. We didn't want to explain to someone whom we saw every day why Great Auntie So-and-so, whom we hadn't seen for twenty years and was presumed buried long ago, had been invited instead. This decision was further made for us when we selected our wedding venue. It will come as no surprise to learn that we wanted to get married in the Aviemore area, and found the perfect venue in the form of Drumintoul Lodge on the Rothiemurchus Estate, right on the edge of the northern Cairngorms.

Rothiemurchus is very much a living and working Highland estate. Actively managed and offering stunning landscapes, it forms part of the Cairngorms National Park. At its heart is one of the largest remaining tracts of natural forest anywhere in Britain, hosting a huge variety of wildlife. This ancient Caledonian Forest is of course just one part of the wild landscape, with lochs, rivers, glens and mountains complementing each other beautifully. This unique and beautiful place is owned, managed and cared for by the Grants of Rothiemurchus, as it has been for generations. A former Victorian shooting lodge on the Rothiemurchus Estate, Drumintoul Lodge is situated in a beautiful setting with stunning views and several cosy rooms with roaring log fires. It was the perfect wedding venue.

May is, in my humble opinion, the best month of the year in Scotland. Spring is definitely in the air, the weather tends to be warm and settled, the midges have not generally made their presence felt yet, and there is seemingly endless daylight available. There is generally snow still lying on the highest mountains, giving the whole environment a wonderful mix of colours and light.

And so it was that on 28th May 2011, Ellen and I got married. Back in Nepal, we had wondered whether it was all just the effects of altitude, but apparently not. However, I'm sure I read we choose our partner based on smell - now that may well have been a factor at the end of those three weeks in Nepal without a shower!

It was an incredibly special day, a wonderful venue (with red squirrels playing in the spring sunshine outside the windows) and a rare opportunity for family members to be in the same place at the same time, something which seems to become increasingly difficult to accomplish as you progress through life. Ellen looked beautiful in her dress. The other ladies present had not, however, thought to discuss their colour schemes with one another, meaning some of the colour photos from the day were "Technicolor" to put it politely! Luckily it was nothing that applying a sepia finish to the photos couldn't sort out. My father and good friend Ian, from Cardiff days, both did me proud with the preparations on the day to try and make me look vaguely respectable. Getting my smart kilt to look right from just the photo on the box was akin to assembling a flat-packed cabinet bearing the immortal but terrifying phrase, "Easy home assembly, no tools required".

Ian is a good friend and generally manages to make a couple of trips up to Scotland each year to go hill walking with me. The sort of friend you can go months without speaking to, yet when you get together again, it's as if you had never been apart. On the hill, conversations over the years have ranged from "the etiquette of the urinal" to "how much rainfall would it take to fill up Loch Tay?" A very clever man, intrigued by the unique ecology of the semi-permanent snow patches of the Cairngorms, he has also been a willing "guinea pig" for me on many occasions when I have been preparing for an assessment. Ian was also the first person to point out to me that, in the nicest possible way, I was very good at finding lunch spots, for one person. If I was to become good at leading groups in the hills, I might need to adjust my auto-finding ability to seek out clusters of boulders to sit on, not just single ones. Lesson number one!

Ian's love of the Cairngorms was well demonstrated on this, the most special of days, when he was spotted gazing longingly out of the window at Braeriach, looking resplendent as ever with the remains of the winter snows still clinging to its high corries, and a fresh dusting of overnight snow lying on the plateau, glinting invitingly in the May sunshine. My mother sidled up to him and with a glint in her eye said, "Go on, admit it, you'd rather be up there, wouldn't you?" Ever the diplomat, Ian spluttered an unconvincing response along the lines that no, he would much rather be inside on a sunny day in May. Ian loves the Cairngorms too. He is a great friend.

Now married, the serious business of getting back to the hills could begin in earnest!

Chapter 14

An Adventure In The Andes

A trip to Bolivia as part of an organised expedition with a group leader followed later that summer. This was a very generous wedding gift to me from one of my sisters and her husband. Ellen didn't fancy this particular trip, but was quite happy for me to go on my own, understanding that climbing in the greater ranges is greatly affected by the seasons, and also that opportunities to do such things must not be turned down. Happily, I returned safely and we were able to enjoy a wonderful trip to the USA together the following year, celebrating our wedding on a proper holiday.

Unsurprisingly, Bolivia turned out to be quite an experience! Very different to Nepal, it was wonderful to get stuck in to another adventure in the greater ranges. Even getting to Bolivia was quite an undertaking, involving a long flight to São Paulo in Brazil, a second flight to Santa Cruz in Bolivia, and a final flight to La Paz. The airport at La Paz (El Alto) is infamous due to its altitude of just over 4,000 m! The highest international airport in the world, it is legendary for making you puff and pant a bit when removing your luggage from the carousel. However, I was spared this particular early test of altitude as the airline had lost my baggage. Luckily for me, I was reunited with it later. Situated on the Altiplano (literally "high plain", the most extensive area of high plateau on Earth outside Tibet and where the Andes are at their widest), El Alto, quite literally, takes your breath away.

La Paz itself sits in a bowl-like depression surrounded by the high mountains of the Altiplano. Despite being in a bowl, it is still very high (c. 3,600 m), so careful acclimatisation is required straight away. In practice, this means taking the first few days very slowly and enjoying some sightseeing before venturing higher. This was hardly a hardship, as we enjoyed some time exploring La Paz, as well as taking a trip to Lake Titicaca, an enormous body of water straddling the border of Bolivia with Peru. The size of Lake Titicaca makes for a surreal experience as being beside it is more akin to being by the sea than by a lake, yet it sits at an altitude of c. 3,800 m. We enjoyed a short boat ride from Copacabana on the Bolivian shores of Lake Titicaca to the Isla del Sol, the spiritual centre of the Andean world where the Inca people believed the sun and the moon were created and where the Inca dynasty was born. Scattered with Inca ruins, inhabited by traditional Aymara communities and with views stretching across the deep blue waters to the snow-capped peaks of the Andes, it was a magical experience.

Acclimatising nicely, it was time to head up, and into Bolivia's stunningly beautiful Cordillera Real. Our sightseeing had been very interesting and had given us some unique insights into the fascinating history and culture of Bolivia and the Andes. It was also an important part of the acclimatisation process, having arrived in the country at such a high altitude. However, it was wonderful finally to be up in the mountains and to settle into expedition life once again.

Trekking from the trailhead took us to Condoriri Base Camp, our home for the next five nights. It was a pleasant location, situated on a very flat piece of ground and surrounded on three sides by towering peaks. It was close to a small lake and, with burros and llamas wandering in the arid landscape and glaciated high mountains in the background, there could be no doubt we were in the Andes. Condoriri, or, to give it its proper name, La Cabeza de Cóndor (the Condor's Head), is a strikingly beautiful mountain, bearing more than a passing resemblance to a condor with outstretched wings. This particular mountain was not on our itinerary, but Condoriri Base Camp was situated conveniently for two of our intended peaks, and it was fabulous to see Condoriri at such close quarters. Now at an altitude of *c.* 4,600 m, the process of acclimatising whilst preparing for the climbs ahead continued. I felt pretty comfortable with this, drawing on the valuable experience I had gained in Nepal. I even had my little bag of orange-flavoured powder to make my water more palatable.

During the first couple of days we made an ascent of our first peak, Pico Austria (5,100 m). This non-glaciated peak was a fine viewpoint and a lovely warm-up for what lay ahead. Gazing from the summit across a great tangle of glaciers and snow-capped peaks I wondered how many (or how few) of the visible peaks had actually been climbed. In no mad rush, our group made a leisurely descent back to base camp and enjoyed the afternoon sun. Located as base camp was, surrounded by high peaks, once the sun disappeared for the day it got very cold very quickly! Just as in Nepal, extensive use was made of my cosy down sleeping bag during periods of inactivity. The next day we headed up from base camp to a nearby glacier to refresh the skills we would need for safe glacial travel. A welcome rest day followed, taking a short hike to a small hill just above base camp, once again "tricking" the body into thinking you are higher than you really are, so your body works harder to deal with it. The combination of "climbing high, sleeping low" for consecutive days is a tried and tested approach to acclimatisation and I was feeling good, ready for the 3 a.m. alarm call the next day.

As I woke in the freezing cold Andean morning, I quickly remembered where I was. I was excited. Today we were going to attempt Pequeño Alpamayo (5,370 m), said to be a smaller version of its eponymous Peruvian neighbour. I knew it was a stunning peak as I had seen photos of it before the trip. The peak itself was not visible from our base camp. In all honesty, and despite the fact we would be attempting at least one 6,000 m peak later in the trip, Pequeño Alpamayo was the one I really wanted to summit. Height isn't everything! Mountaineering is tough, physically and mentally, and just like anything in life, you need to be passionate about your objectives, fired up and ready to have a go. Yet it is important to remember that, when in the mountains, you are a mere speck in a hostile environment with many objective dangers. Just because I was climbing as part of an organised trip where I was not the leader did not mean I should leave my brain in the tent. I had certainly been inspired by the promise of fabulous mountaineering in Bolivia and, once again, I was finding tremendous fulfilment in this most beautiful of landscapes.

It was just a short walk from base camp to the glacier which we were to climb initially, so we elected to put on our harnesses and helmets straight away. It was an odd sight, walking in the pitch black, with our headlamps piercing the darkness as we made our way along the feint path heading towards the glacier. The only drawback of walking with a harness on, when it would perhaps be better off in your rucksack until needed, is the "clink, clink" of karabiners hitting each other. Arriving suddenly at the toe (lowest point) of the glacier, we stopped to rope up in the dark.

The overall leader of our group was working alongside several local mountain guides, each of whom took charge of a pair of clients. Thus, each rope team consisted of three climbers. Stepping on to the glacier in the dark, it quickly became apparent this was going to be a tough day. The ice was bullet-hard and covered with a thin layer of fresh snow, meaning it was necessary to really kick in with each step to ensure the crampons gripped properly. However, getting into a smooth and steady rhythm, we made good progress, working our way up the glacier and weaving around several large crevasses. Eventually, the angle eased as we bypassed a subsidiary summit, before leaving the snow as we reached the top of a rocky ridge, which we would shortly descend.

It was just beginning to get light and, as we stopped for a few moments to catch our breath, I gazed out across an incredible jumble of high peaks as the Andean skyline turned bright orange. Just as in Nepal, it was odd to think back over the last couple of hours, plodding uphill in the dark, not really realising just how much progress we were making. Yet, suddenly, we seemed to be level with the mountains, on them rather than looking up at them. It was stunning.

It was here we saw the summit ridge of Pequeño Alpamayo for the first time - a beautiful steep narrow ridge leading to a perfect summit pyramid of snow at Alpine grade AD (assez difficile - fairly difficult). Suddenly I was very glad to be roped up to an experienced Bolivian mountain guide.

Our route continued, down the rocky ridge which was pleasant scrambling terrain (in crampons!), before meeting the snow once again, at the start of the summit ridge. We started up, placing our ice axes before kicking our crampons in to the hard snow. Upwards, upwards, and slowly upwards, the ridge was in perfect condition, probably about Scottish grade II, but in a very exposed situation. Keeping well to the left to avoid the enormous cornice, the angle eventually eased. A few more paces and I was stood on the top of Pequeño Alpamayo alongside my local Bolivian mountain guide and the other member of our rope team. Wow! The sun was now creeping up in the sky and in every direction there were snow-capped peaks set against the deep blue sky. It was an incredible panorama and definitely worth the 3 a.m. start. I was on top of the peak I had gazed longingly at in books before leaving the UK, and I was not disappointed. What a beautiful mountain.

Hugs, handshakes and photos done, it was time for "lunch", even though it was only about 9 a.m. Then, the reality that we had to reverse the entire outward route to return to base camp entered our minds, and we started down. It was hot by now, with the sun high in the sky. I was so glad my salopettes were black! Still, by the time we had negotiated the summit ridge and the rocky ridge in reverse and were back at the top of the glacier which would take us almost back to camp, at least the sun had softened the top of the glacier a little. This was very welcome as it meant a bit less "stomping" was required. Weaving back around the crevasses, we eventually emerged at the toe of the glacier, where the rope came off and we wandered, wearily but happily, back to base camp and our tents. Stripping off our kit, it was lovely to take advantage of the afternoon sun to give it an airing, snoozing contentedly in our sleeping bags before dinner and bed. I was very happy.

The following day it was time to move on, and as the llamas were readied for their task of transporting our overnight bags back down to the trailhead, our group took a final look around at the magnificent scenery around Condoriri Base Camp. It had been an excellent few days and we had enjoyed our first taste of climbing in Bolivia, but now it was time to trek back down to the trailhead. There, we were met by a bus which drove us round to the base of Huayna Potosi (6,088 m), our next objective at Alpine grade PD. We spent a night in the Refugio Casa Blanca, a lodge at 4,800 m, before trekking up to "high camp", the Campo Alto Roca hut at *c.* 5,200 m. Spirits were high amongst our team members. We were all well acclimatised by now and were looking forward to tomorrow when we would be up at 3 a.m. for another "Alpine start". A relaxing holiday it was not! As I hung my helmet with attached headlamp next to my bunk and settled down to sleep, I took one last look out of the window - we would be heading up there tomorrow. This was my chance to climb my second 6,000 m peak.

The following morning was cold and clear and, as the hut was located right next to the glacier, we roped up from the word go. As this climb was less technical than Pequeño Alpamayo, each rope team now consisted of three clients with either the overall leader of our group or a local mountain guide. The initial parts of the climb were generally straightforward, consisting of easy snow slopes with odd steeper sections. However, in the dark and weaving around large crevasses, it was certainly quite atmospheric. It was also very cold and I remember, just before it started to get light, I was really starting to feel as if I needed the sun to come up. I knew that would provide some much-needed warmth.

Once again, when the sun did come up, it came as quite a surprise to see just where we were. Close by, the summit ridge of Huayna Potosi was to our left, and we were currently skirting it before we would eventually tackle it from a different angle. To the right and straight ahead lay that now-familiar skyline of jagged peaks and glaciers stretching as far as the eye could see. It was an incredible place to be and, given our excellent progress so far, we were nearly there!

The exposed and narrow north ridge was quite a place - not somewhere to be if you weren't confident of your ability in crampons. My rope team, however, made short work of this challenge, enjoying the airy exposure and safe in the hands of our local guide. Very shortly, we arrived at the top of Huayna Potosi, where the famous "snow mushroom" greeted us. We were absolutely elated. This was my first Andean 6,000 m peak, and yet another stunning summit.

Turning and beginning to descend the exposed ridge, I looked out across the Andes, now spread at my feet. There are no words to describe just how beautiful it was. The strange joy of mountaineering once again crept over me. I looked back towards the summit where we had been just minutes before. It was no longer visible. The moment had passed, but I would never forget it. It was too precious an experience to be forgotten, ever.

Returning all the way back to the Refugio Casa Blanca, where the bus had dropped us off a couple of days previously, made for a long day. Yet that did little to dampen spirits as we made our way back to La Paz, showers, and dinner.

We headed back into the mountains after a rest day in La Paz, aiming to climb Illimani (6,439 m). Unfortunately for me, I managed to become a little sick so enjoyed the warm embrace of my sleeping bag at base camp whilst some of the team were on the mountain. I was not unduly upset, however, as it had been a phenomenal trip. I had experienced some fabulous aspects of South American culture and climbed three wonderful mountains whilst enjoying spectacular Andean scenery. As far as I was concerned, I would be heading home having had an amazing trip.

Once again, I had learnt loads from the experience. I noted many times the way our leader worked, seemingly effortlessly, with the wide range of local support staff, from mountain guides to drivers, and from cooks to *arrieros* (muleteers - as in Morocco, people who use pack animals [typically burros or llamas in South America] to transport camping gear, food and other kit when trekking to base camps). I say "seemingly effortlessly" because much later I would come to realise the huge amount of work involved in preparing to lead a group on a multi-day trip, even in Scotland.

The group members were quite an experienced bunch of mountaineers and between us we had ascents of Lobuche East (me!), Mera Peak and Ama Dablam, and much other experience besides, including in Ecuador, Iceland and elsewhere. My tent-mate and I had got on extremely well (although I didn't end up marrying this one) and looked out for each other throughout the trip. "Buddying up" is a very altruistic thing to do and in my experience seems to occur quite naturally within a group. It is comforting to support each other through the highs and lows of life on expedition. This can be for very practical things, such as not relying only on yourself to listen out for the 3 a.m. alarm call on summit day, but also just keeping an eye on each other and checking they're doing OK with regards how they're feeling, acclimatising, eating and drinking etc. By now I was pretty used to the whole acclimatisation process. I found it comforting that, to date at least, I had managed to acclimatise successfully and in a reasonable time frame to reach the summits of what was now a pleasingly-expanding list of 4-, 5- and 6,000 m peaks in Morocco, Nepal and Bolivia. However, each trip to altitude is different, and each time you "start from scratch". Just because you acclimatise successfully on one occasion is no guarantee of being able to do so subsequently. In his book *View From The Summit*, Sir Edmund Hillary (he and Sherpa Tenzing Norgay are the first two people known to have reached the Summit of Everest, on 29th May 1953) describes how, after climbing Everest, he failed to acclimatise successfully to extreme altitude on Makalu, the world's fifth highest mountain at 8,485 m. My mountaineering exploits are not quite in the same league as these two legends! Yet it does illustrate that if altitude can catch up with somebody of Sir Edmund Hillary's experience, it can catch up with anyone. For me, it was another reminder that if there are things I wanted to achieve in life, I was better off getting on with them rather than delaying, as you never know what's around the corner.

Bolivia is a beautiful and interesting country and I hope to return to South America one day, perhaps to Peru? But for now, it was great to get another "big trip" under my belt and return to Scotland safely, married, and full of red blood cells again.

Chapter 15

Climbing And Biking

I had never really been a climber. I loved being out in the mountains, and certainly enjoyed a bit of scrambling. I was also happy to be guided up routes requiring ropes and harnesses etc., but lacked the personal competence I felt necessary to go climbing independently, let alone be responsible for others. The tastes of "proper mountaineering", as I saw it, which I had enjoyed, spurred me on to get into climbing. Initially the motivation was very much with a view to acquiring technical skills which would enable me to complete "more interesting" routes up mountains i.e. rather than just walking to the top, having the necessary skills to look after myself and a friend on a hard scramble/easy climb. It is this sort of "classic mountaineering" which I find incredibly exciting. Summer scrambles and easy winter climbs on some of the UK's classic mountains may be low grade by climbing standards, but take you in to some incredible mountain scenery and open up a whole new world of possibilities.

As well as this personal aspiration, I was also keen to develop a broad base of experience and qualifications with a view to my change in profession. Working towards my Single Pitch Award (SPA), an introductory rock climbing qualification which would enable me to supervise novices on single-pitch crags, was therefore high on my list. The SPA has since been renamed to Rock Climbing Instructor (RCI). At that stage, I had a very long way to go.

Ellen had done a little climbing previously, so we decided to go on an introductory rock climbing course together.

This made a nice change as most of my training was done without Ellen who, despite enjoying the outdoors as much as me, has far too much sense to try and make a living out of it. This was also the first course I did after my Summer ML assessment, and the instructor on the climbing course had been one of my assessors. It was nice not to feel under any pressure and to feel like a student again! The instructor's fun and engaging style was superb, managing to find that all-important balance between "pushing" to extend our skill levels but not to the extent of our getting scared, keeping us safe at all times. It can be a fine line! Once again, in addition to the more overt hard skills, I found myself making mental notes of some of these vital "soft skills" which I would find useful in my own future career.

Over the course of the week we enjoyed ourselves immensely, getting a firm grounding in single-pitch rock climbing at Kingussie Crag, Cummingston, Redhythe and Duntelchaig. Chasing the sun around to find dry rock to climb on was also an appealing aspect of rock climbing I hadn't really considered before.

Somewhat inevitably, I loved rock climbing. It isn't something which comes naturally to me at all, and I wonder how much of that is an age thing? It is very "all absorbing". When concentrating on making the next sequence of moves, looking for the next potential rest spot, scoping ahead for where you might place the next piece of protection etc., there is no space in the head for anything else. In that sense, it is similar to navigating in the mountains in poor conditions. Both offer great mental workouts which make you forget about any other worries in life.

Whilst all this was going on, Ellen had also corrupted me back to the ways of cycling regularly. Ellen was a keen time trialist who had been the 5th and 6th fastest woman in Scotland in 2006 and 2008 respectively. My experience on a bike had lapsed considerably in recent years, apart from fixing the odd puncture for friends during my undergraduate days, so I was a little rusty, to say the least. I might have been fastest to the biscuit cupboard, but in anything sporting I am one of life's plodders, doing nothing fast but able to sustain physical activity for a long time.

At this stage, I didn't even own a bike anymore. Down south, my little grey mountain bike which had carried me, so many times, backwards and forwards to the supermarket where I worked, had succumbed to rust from all those bait-digging trips. This meant I had to hire a mountain bike on the odd occasion when I was feeling particularly masochistic, using the bike to access some of the more remote hills for bigger days out in a "bike and hike" day - cycling in, then walking to climb a hill or two before cycling out.

On one day which sticks in the mind, I hired a bike from Braemar, cycled in to the ruins of Geldie Lodge, hid my bike in the heather and climbed the remote Munros of An Sgarsoch and Carn an Fhidhleir. I then returned to Geldie Lodge and cycled back to Braemar. Carn an Fhidhleir is an interesting hill as it sits at the meeting place of Perthshire, Aberdeenshire and Inverness-shire, quite literally in the middle of nowhere. The neighbouring summit of An Sgarsoch was, in times past, a market place where cattle and horses were bought and sold. For days such as this, a bike is invaluable at bringing remote hills within range of a day's walk. All in, that day was a round trip of about 40 miles, 28 miles of which I had cycled and 12 miles of which I had walked. Being a confident rider would open up a whole new range of possibilities for me. The downside is ending up with a sore arse to go with your sore feet at the end of a good day out! Wild camping is, of course, another wonderful way to experience such remote places.

Luckily for me, Ellen had a spare bike (in fact, several spares) and I enjoyed getting back out. Very soon, we were both right back in to our mountain biking. We didn't do anything hard core, just pleasant off-road biking on trails, through forests and across moorland, basically trying to avoid tarmac. It was great, and I also found it to be another good way of keeping fit away from the hills. Climbing hills all the time trashes your knees, yet biking offers a more measured workout, without the constant jarring associated with walking downhill. With the popularity of mountain biking soaring, I registered for my Trail Cycle Leader (TCL) qualification, progressed to owning my own mountain bike once again, and eventually passed my TCL assessment in the autumn of 2012. This was good! I now had my Summer ML as well as my TCL.

In parallel with this, I gradually built up my climbing kit, developing from having just a helmet, harness and rock shoes to having a full lead rack and rope. Ellen and I got out as much as we could, and my progress was helped greatly by attending a three-week-long intensive course in North Wales some years later. This really gave my lead climbing a kick start.

Once again, it was apparent no qualification was going to happen by accident. Ellen and I spent a huge amount of time in the summer before my SPA assessment getting as much mileage at a range of single-pitch crags as we could. As well as personal climbing (I would need to lead routes graded up to Severe during the assessment) and abseiling, it was also important that I practised various setups for working with groups, as well as some of the problem scenarios which might occur. Once again, Ellen was among my willing "guinea pigs"!

There is a saying often applied in military circles, that is, "train hard, fight easy", and I have heard this applied to succeeding with outdoor qualifications on more than one occasion. The idea is that, essentially, the better prepared you are, the easier the assessment will be. At least, that's the theory. There is no way you can ever pre-empt every single scenario which might arise. However, by practising a range of techniques, and by applying some lateral thinking in order to solve a problem you perhaps haven't come across before, you give yourself the best possible chance. There is the additional theory that the more mistakes you make during your preparation, the less likely you are to make the same mistake again, as you will (hopefully!) learn why the mistake occurred and not do it again.

During a day of personal climbing at the Pass of Ballater, Ellen and I were enjoying the sunshine. I had climbed Lime Chimney, an eight-metre climb graded VDiff (Very Difficult, a grade below Severe), and was stood at the top of the crag. There is an excellent selection of anchors here, ranging from mature Scots pine trees to some very obliging boulders. Normally I would have tied in before bringing Ellen up as my second. However, for this scenario, I was going to abseil back down the crag to retrieve the gear I had placed earlier whilst leading the climb, much as if Ellen had decided for whatever reason that she didn't want to climb it after me. It was a good scenario to practise.

Safety first and all that, I arranged an anchor that I was happy to abseil off and connected myself to it with a cow's tail (a short safety line used to connect yourself to an anchor). I was now safe at the top of the crag and Ellen was safe at the bottom of the crag.

Rigging a retrievable abseil, one where the rope can be pulled down after the descent, meant both Ellen and I had to untie from the rope, so it is a good idea to attach the rope to the anchor at the top of the crag before doing so. I would then pull all of the rope up to the top of the crag, find the mid-point of the rope and clip that in to the anchor using a large karabiner. The rope is then thrown down the crag so you end up with two strands of rope reaching all the way to the bottom of the crag, with the rope just passing through, as opposed to being tied to, the karabiner at the top. The initial attachment of the rope to the anchor can then be released, safe in the knowledge that the rope isn't going to disappear down the crag. I would then attach myself to both strands of rope, unclip my cow's tail, abseil down, then pull on either strand of rope to pull the whole rope through.

However, that day I forgot to attach the rope to the anchor before untying from the rope. Most of the rope was still at the bottom of the crag, obviously, and I watched in horror as the rope's own weight pulled it from my grip and accelerated it across the granite slabs and pine needles before flipping it neatly over the edge of the crag. Oops! This was a big mistake!

There I was, clipped in at the top of a climb, but now with no rope with which to abseil back down. Had I been on a multi-pitch route, this would have been a whole lot more serious. Luckily for me, this was a single-pitch venue with ready access between the top and bottom of the crag. I duly unclipped my cow's tail, made my way sheepishly to the bottom of the crag, collected the rope, then carried it back up to the top of the crag and rigged the abseil properly. I abseiled off, retrieving the gear I had placed earlier. I learnt a very valuable lesson that day - always make sure you AND THE ROPE are clipped or tied to the anchor before untying the rope when preparing to abseil. I was glad it happened then rather than on assessment - or worse, on a multi-pitch climb!

I practised, practised and practised until the day of my SPA assessment dawned bright and early. Except it wasn't bright; it was throwing it down. Cummingston was to be the venue for our first morning, and normally the Costa del Moray is somewhat spoilt for weather. Not today though, and so my assessment started, wearing full waterproofs. This reminded me of being back in North Wales.

As is customary, the assessment began with personal climbing, and I duly paired up with a fellow candidate and we went climbing. The idea is to demonstrate personal climbing competency, testing your communication, gear placements, choice of anchors, belaying, personal abseiling etc., and is much like going out climbing with a mate. With water pouring off the rock, the requirement to lead climbs graded Severe was ditched initially, and we enjoyed leading and seconding some climbs graded Diff (Difficult, a grade below Very Difficult) and VDiff in the pouring rain. Eventually the sun did come out to play, and we were suddenly cooking. For me, a quick romp up Staircase Crack, a 12 m climb graded Severe, ticked that box nicely, and after half a dozen routes, mostly in the pouring rain, it was time to move on to the next part of the assessment.

An afternoon in the dry at a local climbing wall was followed by a day at Huntly's Cave. Here, we rigged group abseils, we rigged top and bottom ropes, and we retrieved "stuck" climbers as if our lives depended upon it. It was another nervous wait after two very full days, but another proud day and another massive confidence boost when I was told I had passed my SPA. It was now October 2015.

The change from being a fisheries scientist to an outdoor instructor was never going to happen overnight. Several things needed to fall into place or, more accurately, be engineered to happen. Ellen and I decided to stay living apart during the years when we were first married. This, we reasoned, provided the opportunity to get some financial security behind us while we could both take advantage of having a reliable income. Meanwhile, I would gain as many outdoor qualifications as I could whilst working in a "normal" job. We also knew it is a difficult thing for two people to find work in specialised fields in the same place in a rural location. We would make a clean break at such a time as we felt appropriate, selling both properties to fund our move to the Aviemore area. That was our plan, and we stuck to it.

At this point in late 2015, I was buzzing with what I had achieved in terms of gaining outdoor qualifications. Since passing my Summer ML in 2009, I had added my TCL in 2012 and my SPA in 2015. This meant I was qualified to lead summer hill walking, to supervise rock climbing on single-pitch crags and to lead mountain bike rides within certain constraints of height and remoteness. With three years between each award, this might not seem like meteoric progress, but it was pretty impressive when you consider I didn't work in the outdoor industry yet. Because of this, I really had to push to gain voluntary "shadowing" and other group management experience to progress through the various assessments, typically in my own time and at my own expense.

Ellen had been massively helpful in her efforts to assist where she could, having been subjected to various rescue scenarios (intentionally set up, I might add!) on single-pitch crags and having accompanied me on many wild camping and mountain biking trips. Ellen is also a superb teacher when it comes to bike repair skills. I also had a demanding job in science with increasingly long hours, and I spent extended periods away from home carrying out field work and attending meetings, many of which were overseas. In parallel with my unquestionable desire to work in the outdoors, I was finding my job increasingly stressful as time went on. Coinciding with a period of significant cuts in public spending, it seemed to me there was an ever-increasing workload, diminishing resources and growing uncertainty in the workplace. This was not helped by the fact Ellen and I were spending so much time travelling between our respective homes.

Ellen and I had identified five outdoor qualifications which I could realistically obtain "off my own bat", i.e. ones which I felt were achievable, given sufficient hard work and dedication, before taking the plunge into the outdoor industry. I wanted to commit fully when the time came and not work part-time in the outdoors. I now had three of these qualifications and I was well on my way towards the other two, namely the Winter ML and Climbing Wall Award (CWA), since renamed to Climbing Wall Instructor (CWI). Taken together, I reasoned these five awards would provide me with a diverse set of qualifications to offer potential employers and, importantly, the potential to work year-round. I was satisfied my Winter ML would fall into place nicely once we got to Aviemore, as I would have one of Britain's best winter mountain playgrounds on my doorstep. I had completed my training several years previously and was well on my way to assessment.

Our "escape" plan was coming together nicely. I knew we were about to make the right move.

Chapter 16

Big Bag Day

One of my brothers-in-law, Fiona's husband of Ford KA-funding fame, has come to mean a great deal to me over recent years. Married to Fiona since 2004, he is a man who doesn't suffer fools, gladly or otherwise, yet has the reassuring and non-judgemental tone of one much older and wiser. By his own admission he has less patience than a man who has drunk ten pints of lager and been told to stand in the queue for the gents for two hours. Patient he is not (fitting in well with the rest of our family!), yet at the same time he has an uncanny ability to stand back from any situation and view it with ruthless objectivity and pragmatism. Often his opening gambit to any given problem will be along the lines of, "OK, no one's died [usually they hadn't]; this can be sorted out." Sharp as a stick, and incredibly astute with respect to financial matters in particular, he is a firm advocate that people make decisions of their own free will, often in full knowledge of the likely consequences, and have to live with the outcomes. Fair to say he has little time for people, yet dotes on his various pet cats which have come and gone over the years. Often misunderstood, his very black-and-white view of the world can rub people up the wrong way. Yet beneath the skin is a wonderful, compassionate and loving human being, only with your best interests at heart, despite having experienced things in life which no human should ever have to endure. He is a wonderful man, brother (to me at least), loving husband to Fiona, food supplier and source of warmth (to various cats) and friend to many. Dishing out the best bear hugs in the business, and cooking an awesome Christmas dinner, I love him very much, and not only for his Christmas dinners.

Now retired, his professional career was interesting and varied. Initially a teacher, and a very good one at that, he had moved into investigative journalism. His latter career, working largely for himself, was exciting but unpredictable, yet offered him a far better lifestyle than the daily grind. It was a lifestyle choice he and Fiona made (with her also moving out of the teaching profession), and they made it work, giving them opportunities to spend significant periods abroad in the sunshine, freed from the shackles of an employer but lacking the certainty of a monthly pay cheque. In broad terms, this mirrored my proposed move into the outdoor industry from a settled job. Knowing they had made it work for them inspired me and Ellen on our journey.

He had regaled me many times with the tale of his last day in teaching when, on a matter of principle, he had famously taken in a big bag, walked in to the head's office and announced his imminent departure. "You wouldn't do that," said the head. "Watch me," came the reply, returning to his classroom for the last time to sweep the contents of his desk into the big bag. My departure from the workplace was going to be slightly more diplomatic, but my own "big bag day" was fast approaching.

Early in 2016, Ellen and I set the wheels in motion which would ultimately result in our living together in Aviemore. We knew what needed to happen and that with a bit of luck and good timing, it was perfectly feasible. Nonetheless, it was a daunting list: selling two properties; buying one property; leaving two jobs, and securing work in the same place where we bought the property. That would take care of the morning, but what would we do in the afternoon?! We were also aware that, much as we wanted to live together as a married couple, and much as we wanted to move to the Aviemore area and change our working arrangements, this was a pretty big thing we were doing. Any one of the things we needed to achieve had the potential to be extremely stressful, so we also needed to be mindful of achieving all of this without falling out! After all, I needed that tent in one piece.

My flat sale was very straightforward as I had found a private buyer. The plan was that, after finishing my job I would move up to Ellen's in Inverurie for a short time so we could complete the sale of her place before going across to Aviemore together. Ellen, meanwhile, had largely taken control of securing a place in Aviemore. I was involved in a lengthy piece of fieldwork on the west coast during the spring of 2016, which meant I was out of commission for several weeks. However, we knew we were looking for a place somewhere in what we often refer to as the Newtonmore to Grantown-on-Spey corridor. Essentially we would not rule out anything in the villages of Newtonmore, Kingussie, Kincraig, Boat of Garten, Nethybridge or Grantown-on-Spey, but Aviemore was top of the list due to its central location in the Highlands, the good access afforded to other areas, and the fact it is so close to fabulous mountains, forests, rivers and lochs for walking, biking, mountaineering and climbing.

As well as its excellent location for outdoor work and play, we also knew Aviemore would be an easy place to live in from a practical point of view, with excellent day-to-day facilities including shops, a doctors' surgery, a dentist and an optician, a garage, car mechanic and filling station, and a post office, as well as plenty of cafés, hotels, restaurants and takeaways, and of course, a mainline railway station and a good bus service. It was also just a short distance from the coast and an airport at Inverness. Looking ahead, we also saw Aviemore as being perfectly amenable to our likely needs in retirement, having good community services in addition to those benefits mentioned above. What's not to like?

Several viewings later, and we eventually got to the point of a second viewing on a house in Aviemore. I came along for this second viewing. The house would need some work, but the location and everything else about it were just about perfect. Quite frankly I think I would have bought a garden shed to live in if I had a view of the Cairngorms from my window, but fortunately Ellen's slightly more pragmatic approach ensured more practical matters were considered fully. I do love the fact I can see Braeriach, Cairn Gorm and Bynack More from the end of my road!

The nature of planning foreign trips also meant Ellen and I had booked, months previously, a trip to Iceland for the middle of June, an arrangement made before finally nailing down job-leaving and house-moving dates. Cancelling our trip to Iceland was never considered and, after all the shenanigans associated with viewing houses and making arrangements regarding the imminent sale of my flat and Ellen's bungalow, we were glad to be "off the radar" for a week. This was my second visit to Iceland, but unlike my first visit which was to attend a fisheries conference, it was wonderful to explore some of the country's incredible landscape. Joining as part of a group on an organised trip, we climbed a number of smaller mountains during the first few days. The names of these mountains make pronouncing the names of Munros in the Northwest Highlands seem like child's play! Syđstasúla, Mount Botnssúlur (1,093 m) and Svinafellsfjall (*c.* 800 m) were climbed, the first offering a very Scotland-like experience on an interesting route involving some steep slopes, a narrow ridge and the crossing of some non-permanent snowfields. Just to spice it up a bit, the rock on the ridge was often "less than perfect", a polite way of saying handholds would come away from the mountain with alarming ease once touched! And if that wasn't enough, the loose stones sitting on the solidified lava slopes were more akin to climbing up a steep slope covered in ball bearings. It was great fun though, and so windy. We felt right at home.

The climax of the trip was an ascent of the 1,875 m peak Hrútsfjallstindar at Alpine grade F (facile - easy), a stunning and shapely glaciated peak located on the rim of the Vatnajökull Glacier, Europe's largest icecap. Climbed from sea level, this was a big day by any measure, and with Lady Luck on our side when it came to the weather, we were blessed with a bluebird day and views to die for.

The first day back after Iceland, Ellen secured a buyer for her place in Inverurie, and our offer on the Aviemore house was accepted. We were all set. Returning to my job for three short days felt a little surreal, to say the least. All I really had to do was tidy up some loose ends and make sure everything was in order. As had become customary on anyone's last day, I appreciated gathering with all my colleagues on my final afternoon. Coffee and cake were enjoyed and a presentation made to me on behalf of my colleagues, who'd had a generous whip-round for a leaving gift. The shape of the envelope quickly dispelled my fear it might be a pet salmon. It was too flat - but, a plaice maybe? I was delighted to discover the envelope did in fact contain gift vouchers for a well-known outdoor retailer. Perfect! These would come in very handy and were much appreciated.

Over the years, I had fulfilled a variety of roles and worked with a number of groups within the laboratory. As I commented at my presentation, "I've been in more groups than Bon Jovi!" Ever the diplomat, what had once been one of my frustrations, I turned into a positive on this occasion, mentioning that because of this, I had worked with the vast majority of the laboratory staff at one point or another. It was true, and it was nice at this point to view this as a positive. They were a good bunch and I would be taking away many fond memories. Up until now, connections with the laboratory had been the one constant during my time in Scotland, and cutting loose from it overnight was always going to feel a bit strange. But I was also old enough and ugly enough to know the laboratory would continue to function perfectly well without me. We all like to think of ourselves as being indispensable, but I was under no illusions. Late on my last afternoon I took the opportunity to pop around a few of the offices to chat individually with selected folk, particularly those whom I wanted to thank personally for their help over the years. At 5 p.m. I drove down the laboratory driveway for the last time, as I had done so many times before, passing beautiful Loch Faskally as I went.

I am sure there were some who expected me to be ringing up the laboratory a few weeks or months later, pleading for my job back. In discussions with people before leaving, it had become polite for me at least to acknowledge the suggestion of, "Oh well, if it doesn't work out, you can always fall back on your qualifications and get a job back in science." Cheeky beggars! I never considered this possibility. Partly this would have been down to personal pride, an admission of failure. Partly it has never been necessary. But partly I was also aware that science and people move on quickly. It would not take long being "out of the game" to be completely out of touch with so many aspects of the work, so I very much doubt I would have been able just to "slot back in" to science, even if I had ever wanted to. Heaven forbid!

I drove down the A9 back to my flat in Birnam for the last time. There was no going back now. It was 29th June 2016. It was my "big bag day".

Chapter 17

Moving On

The following day I waited nervously for my solicitor to ring and tell me that the sale of my flat had gone through successfully. Sure enough, all was well, and I left my lovely little flat in Birnam for the last time and headed north.

As planned, I moved up to Inverurie for a few weeks as the timings made that easier. It was a busy period, making final preparations for moving to Aviemore, but I still found time for a few days out in the hills. One of my favourites incorporated the grade 1 scramble up the Stuic, a fine ridge in a spectacular setting to the south of Lochnagar, high above Loch nan Eun. A quick romp across Carn a' Choire Bhoidheach and Carn an t-Sagairt Beag before returning through the beautiful Ballochbuie Forest completed a great day out.

Ellen finished her job and on 19th August 2016, we drove across to Aviemore, accompanied by a removal van containing all our belongings. Enjoying fish and chips in Aviemore that evening, we reflected on the enormity (or stupidity!) of what we had just done. We had left two good jobs of our own free will and had sold two properties which were nicely decorated and in good working order. We now lived in Aviemore and were mortgage free, but now had no income, and a new home in need of renovation.

The next six months were very hard work as we had a lot of jobs to do in our new home. Despite the temptation to go out and play, and sod's law meant it was a beautiful autumn, we were very disciplined and stuck at the jobs, reasoning that if we stopped it could end up taking years to get the house up together. Not for the first time, our dedication to hard work and continuing with a plan paid off and, come Christmas time, we were the proud owners of our lovely little home in Aviemore, nicely done up and ready for our new adventure.

So there we were, January 2017, and ... what now? I needed some outdoor work! I had my Summer ML, SPA, and TCL. Early in 2017 I would add my Winter ML and CWA to this list.

It would be somewhat inappropriate at this stage simply to mention in passing the Winter ML without a second thought. As alluded to earlier, achieving this award was the hardest qualification of any kind I have ever obtained, and is the one of which I am most proud. The award builds on the skills learnt through the Summer ML scheme, and is for those wanting to lead groups of hill walkers in the UK under winter conditions. Despite wanting to do the award anyway, it had also become clear to me that in order to work year-round in Scotland, this was an essential qualification for me to obtain.

My preparations had begun many years ago, perhaps without even realising it, beginning with those first tentative steps into Scotland's winter mountains a decade previously. By the time I completed my Summer ML in the autumn of 2009, I already had "enough" personal winter experience to register for my Winter ML, and attend the training course early in 2010, the first available winter. (The Summer ML is a pre-requisite for the Winter ML, and registration for the winter scheme is not available until you have passed your Summer ML.) I say "enough" personal winter experience in that way, because all the criteria set down as minimums for proceeding through the various qualification schemes are exactly that - minimum requirements - and having more is always beneficial. This applies particularly to the minimum requirements for proceeding to the Winter ML assessment, as the greater breadth of experience you have gained, the more likely you are to have a successful outcome at assessment, with the term "Winter Quality Mountain Day" used as a measure of experience. It is also fair to say that going in to the Winter ML training course fresh off the back of my successful Summer ML assessment was something of a reality check - the Winter ML was a big step up.

My approach to the Winter ML was very similar to that for the other outdoor qualifications I had completed. I was going out in winter a lot anyway, so experience was gained rapidly, both personal as well as leading other individuals or small groups on an informal basis. Simply going out into the winter mountains regularly and honing my skills was incredibly worthwhile and naturally covered many areas of the syllabus such as navigation, avalanche awareness and route selection and planning, as well as generally getting slick looking after myself and making decisions in a harsh environment. Areas of the syllabus which did need particular focus and time devoted specifically to them were security on steep ground and basic skills instruction.

Once again, Ellen was a very willing "guinea pig". It can be surprisingly difficult to convince anyone they really do want to wander up in to the back of a corrie on a winter's day, only to practise building snow anchors, or work on the finer points of demonstrating snowcraft or digging emergency shelters. Generally, people would much rather go walking or climbing, or even stay at home in the warm. But these focussed practice days proved absolutely invaluable. The acquisition of winter climbing experience so Winter ML candidates are comfortable and confident on grade I terrain also required some focus. I soloed many grade I climbs, but enjoyed taking Ellen out too. On the first of these occasions, I managed to convince her that E Gully in Corrie Fee would make a gentle introduction to grade I gullies, being just 60 m in length with an easy walk in, and with a generally forgiving exit at the top of the climb. It was a great day, but Ellen was quick to point out that although the climb itself may be only 60 m in length, according to the guidebook, it required a considerable effort just to get to the bottom of the 60 m climb! I had to buy the tea that night.

My general resistance to committing to my Winter ML assessment was, in my opinion at least, fully justified. My rather lame excuse of, "Oh, I still need more experience," could be paraphrased as, "I don't want to fail because I don't want to have to come back and re-do the expedition!" More about that later. Nonetheless, the preparations over many years paid off, and I built up a good bank of experience. When Ellen and I had finally taken the plunge and got ourselves to Aviemore, my preparations for assessment were able to move up several gears as I now lived with the Cairngorms on my doorstep, and we had just about finished renovating our new home by Christmas 2016. There were no more excuses, so I went for my assessment in February 2017, but not before twisting my ankle quite badly.

It was February 1st 2017, about two weeks until my assessment. I had traversed around the rim of the northern corries of Cairn Gorm and my logbook reveals it was a day of light snow, extremely poor visibility and strong winds. Nothing extraordinary there! There were great sheets of water ice on the plateau and, looking back, I suspect there had been a thaw of lying snow up to summit levels, followed by a hard freeze. Much of the snow had melted to water which had then frozen into solid ice. I had stood on the top of Cairn Lochain with my crampons on, where I noted the light snow was beginning to create some nasty conditions underfoot - rocks were becoming partially covered by a thin layer of snow, surrounded by sheet ice. I had studied the map, working out a strategy to get down to the top of the Lochain ridge whilst giving the top of the "twin burns" a wide berth. A dog leg to be proud of later, I had located the top of the Lochain ridge successfully and, as the cloud had also lifted, all I had to do was wander down the ridge. I had done this so many times before, crossing the stream flowing out from Coire an Lochain, then skirting back round to the main ski-centre car park. Nothing could go wrong now, could it?

Setting off down the ridge, I suddenly placed one of my crampons awkwardly on a rock which was partially covered in snow. The crampon twisted instantly as I weighted that foot, and my ankle twisted with it. The sharp pain which followed made me see stars (and not in a good way, as at Lobuche East Base Camp) and my immediate reaction was to think I had broken my ankle. Sitting down with my back against a large boulder, all I wanted to do was close my eyes and go to sleep. With enough presence of mind to know this was a really silly idea, I opened my eyes and told myself off for not being more careful, and realised quite quickly that my ankle was not broken. It hurt, no doubt about it, but I could move my foot, and in the great balance of things, the pain was certainly bearable. Knowing I could still move my foot was comforting, but I had to try hard to resist the urge to take off my boot and socks and have a look. I felt sure my foot would be swelling up, and I feared I might be unable to put the socks and boot back on the foot again. Keen to keep moving, as it wasn't the warmest day ever, I managed to get myself back up on my feet, and by weighting my "good" foot and leaning on my walking pole on my "bad" side, I managed to hobble back to the car park. In fact, by the time I neared the car park, I was almost looking like I knew how to walk!

Luckily for me, it turned out to be a twisted ankle which sorted itself out over the next couple of days. I was still getting the odd twinge from it on my assessment a couple of weeks later, sufficient that I felt it necessary to let my assessors know, but luckily it turned out fine. As with things which had gone wrong before other assessments, it was a timely reminder that switching off, even for a second, is a bad idea. Whenever anything goes wrong, it is usual to go back over events and question why things went wrong. Self-reflection is an important part of the learning process. Should I still have had my crampons on at that point? Yes, I should, my decision making in this regard was fine. Should I have been placing my feet more carefully, looking out for rogue stones lying half embedded in ice, half covered in snow? Yes, I should. I had even noted this earlier in the day! I had switched off for a split second, knowing I had done the taxing parts of the day, knowing I was nearly back safely, and that had been enough to injure myself. On a different day, further from safety, in worse weather conditions, the outcome could well have been much more severe. Another useful learning experience and more mental notes made for when leading a group in similar conditions in future.

The assessment came, taking a broadly similar format to that of the Summer ML, i.e. for the first two days we returned to base each evening, before heading out on the third day for a three-day, two-night expedition. The expedition is a tough experience, and is deliberately meant to be so. The whole point is not just to "survive" the experience, but to maintain yourself in a physical and, equally as important, mental condition so you can continue to operate as a safe and effective leader in what is usually a harsh environment. Living in a snow hole, a large purpose-built shelter dug in to a deep bank of stable snow, is a surreal experience. Very different to digging and using an emergency shelter, snow holing is a planned overnight stay, so cooking and sleeping kit etc. is carried. Digging a snow hole is not easy. On my assessment it took four of us six hours to dig!

Out and about on the Cairngorm Plateau, day and night, you are certainly put through your paces as a Winter ML candidate, but as with most things in life, the harder it is, the greater the sense of achievement when you come out on the other side successfully. My fellow candidates and I were in a jovial mood as we made our way down Windy Ridge on the final morning, which was a Friday. We bumped in to a fairly elderly couple making their way up, who asked us excitedly, "Did you make it all the way to the top of Cairn Gorm?" When we replied we had been out, intentionally, since Wednesday morning, they seemed a little bewildered and that was the end of that conversation. The looks on their faces suggested, "Why would anyone in their right mind do that?" Why indeed?! To this day, and the subject of a magazine article I once wrote, my favourite line in the Winter ML syllabus is, "Above all, the experience [of a Winter Quality Mountain Day] should lead to feelings of accomplishment and satisfaction, even if enjoyment may occasionally be questionable!" Enjoyment may well have been questionable at times, but the feelings of accomplishment and satisfaction were massive when I was told, later that afternoon, I had passed my Winter ML assessment.

Hurray! I was absolutely over the moon. From a personal perspective, it had been a long, tough journey to achieve this. Suddenly, every time I had practised whiteout navigation seemed worthwhile. All those days spent in the midst of a freezing gale with little to see but snow-covered rocks and the inside of a cloud had been worth it. Ellen's help as a willing "guinea pig" on the end of a rope attached to a snow bollard had not been in vain. Oh, and those blue-sky days when we had been able to see nothing but snow-covered peaks from the Cairngorms to Ben Nevis seemed suddenly extra special. From a professional perspective, I was confident this would enable me to lead year-round, knowing the summer season in Scotland can be quite short. I also hoped that, even for summer work, having a higher qualification than was technically necessary might push me towards the top of the pile when it came to dishing out work. There had to be some reward for spending several nights in a snow hole!

With a nice clutch of qualifications in the bag by the end of April 2017, my approaches to outdoor activity providers began. I had always been a little bit apprehensive about this. Would I find enough work? Would I find any work at all? Would it be difficult to persuade providers I was serious about working in the outdoors, given my career to date? CVs were sent, emails were followed up, phone calls were made and more than one cup of coffee was consumed with a potential provider. I was as keen as mustard, had a good range of qualifications, plenty of knowledge of several areas of the Highlands and an intriguing life experience to date.

But more importantly, I had the attitude that no provider owed me anything. Any job market is competitive, and the outdoor industry is no different. There are plenty of really well-qualified and experienced people out there, and I was only too aware of that. Still, I thought, you have to start somewhere. If I can snare a few jobs, and start to build up a reputation as someone who is reliable, does a good job and gives the clients a great experience, I'll be well on my way.

As it turned out, there is plenty of work available. What *was* very different from anything I had done before was how available work was advertised. Many job opportunities would appear on Facebook, while a number of outdoor activity providers would add you to a generic mailing list, or have a private Facebook group where they would advertise the latest available opportunities. Other providers would text you offering you a job. If you were available on that day and you wanted it, it was yours. I was entering the world of freelancing.

Work offers started sporadically, but quickly built. As expected, the clichéd "you're only as good as your last job" proved to be accurate, and I started working for several outdoor activity providers, often on hill-based work such as Ben Nevis ascents, Ben Nevis legs of National 3-Peaks Challenges, guided hill walking as far afield as the Lake District, some climbing and winter skills/leading work, and the odd bit of mountain biking to add variety. It was good fun. However, just because outdoor professionals love what we do, I feel it is important to not sell ourselves short when it comes to valuing ourselves and our experience in monetary terms. It takes years of hard work and dedication (not to mention the financial cost) to end up working professionally in any industry, and the outdoors is no different.

At this time, it was also useful to begin learning the finer points of which types of work were the most enjoyable and the most rewarding, and who the prompt paying providers were. I also applied to work for a Scottish adventure travel company, and they were keen to have me on their guiding team. I was offered a few jobs with them in my first season, which I happily accepted, grateful for these typically multi-day chunks of work and keen to impress.

We were living in Aviemore. I was working in the outdoors. Ellen was also successful at finding work and was enjoying her job. We were both enjoying the area together in our spare time. Now was not the time to sit back and relax. If we worked hard we could really get this going.

Chapter 18

The Great Big Mouse Of Ben Nevis

Ben Nevis, often simply referred to as "the Ben", is the UK's highest mountain at 1,345 m, and is a magnet for walkers and climbers from around the world. From the summit it is possible to see half of Scotland spread before you. In the northwest, there is the unmistakable outline of Skye's jagged Black Cuillin. In the east, those in the know can pick out the distinctive profile of Cairn Toul in the Cairngorms, from which the huge bulk of Braeriach can also be identified, a little to the left (north). To the southwest, Loch Linnhe stretches away to Mull and beyond, while closer to hand, the shapely peaks of the Mamores and Glen Coe seem within touching distance. Many more peaks can be identified if you have the time and the inclination, assuming of course the summit is not covered in cloud, which it is for much of the time!

When musing over the origins of the name with clients, I have, on more than one occasion, been asked, "Who was Ben Nevis?" It is probably fair to say that whoever named Ben Nevis was not employed in sales and marketing. The name is an Anglicisation of the Scottish Gaelic *Beinn Nibheis*, *Beinn* meaning mountain and *Nibheis* meaning malicious or venomous. The origins of the name are hotly debated, however, with alternative interpretations including "mountain with its head in the clouds" or "mountain of heaven". I have been up there many times when any one of these descriptions would be perfectly applicable.

The summit plateau is a very serious place, surrounded on almost all sides by steep ground and cliffs. It is perfectly normal for there to be snow on the summit plateau of Ben Nevis until well into the summer. A covering of snow, particularly when accompanied by low cloud, can make route finding and navigation very challenging indeed.

There are, quite literally, many hundreds of ways to ascend Ben Nevis. Many of these are climbing routes, summer and winter, taking impressive lines amid the imposing cliffs of the north face. These cliffs are famous internationally amongst climbers, and here the boundaries of modern climbing are still being pushed. Pleasingly, there are "easier", or more accurately, less technical, routes too, including some excellent scrambles, so with the appropriate skills and experience this incredible setting can be enjoyed by mountaineers and climbers operating across the grade ranges.

Choices for true "walking routes" are more limited, with the mountain track being probably the only route not involving any significant steep ground or scrambling. Many people incorrectly refer to the mountain track as the "tourist track". This is incorrect, and conjures up all the wrong images. Although the "easiest" route up and down Ben Nevis, this should not be underestimated, and a good level of fitness is required, as well as all the usual skills necessary to look after yourself in the mountains if attempted under your own steam. Flip flops are definitely not appropriate! The proper name of the route is in fact the "pony track", following the approximate line of the path once used by those accessing a weather observatory which operated on the summit for 20 years from 1883. And what weather it must have observed! The remains of the observatory are still visible to this day, assuming they are not buried under snow.

For hill walkers with plenty of prior experience on steep and/or exposed ground, and perhaps a little easy scrambling, there are several excellent routes to the top. A popular choice is to climb Carn Mor Dearg (CMD) first, before continuing to Ben Nevis via a long, narrow and rocky ridge, the CMD Arête. There are also routes starting from Steall in Glen Nevis, to the south of Ben Nevis, and an interesting route up via the headwall of Coire Leis.

For many clients, perhaps visiting Scotland on holiday, walking to the top of the UK's highest peak is an obvious objective. The fact that any mountain is "the highest" in - insert place name - continues to be a powerful draw. Ben Nevis also has the advantage over many Scottish mountains in that when clients return home, all their family and friends will have (a) heard of it, and (b) be able to pronounce it, adding further kudos to their achievement. The same may not be applicable had they walked up Braigh Coire Chruinn-bhalgain! This mountain is a fine Munro usually climbed as part of the Beinn a' Ghlo trio, just north of Blair Atholl.

As any number of MLs will tell you, walking up and down Ben Nevis via the pony track with clients is bread and butter work in Scotland. Whether it's a family or couple on holiday, individuals joining a guided group walk, a charity event, a corporate group, or a group undertaking one of the legs of the National 3-Peaks Challenge, this type of work is readily available and can be good fun. It also helps with hill fitness which is obviously important. I need to be fit for my work, and can recall one day when I was expecting a fairly leisurely day with a client, and it turned out he wanted to complete a classic round of six Munros! I was glad I'd had a big breakfast that day. However, I also want to be fit for my time off so I can go and enjoy my own time in the mountains. My work keeps me fit for my time off, and vice versa. I can recall more than one occasion when I have summited Ben Nevis five times in the space of eight days, and you need to be pretty fit to do that. So readily available is the work in fact, that if you want diversity it is important to be selective, as you could probably fill up your diary for the entire summer with little else. Nonetheless, it can be very rewarding. Clients employing the services of a ML for Ben Nevis can be surprisingly nervous, and it reassures them no end if they know they are with someone who is very familiar with the route. Besides which, I am often helping the client to achieve something which is a big deal for *them*. Being part of that achievement makes it special for me too and I try never to downplay their achievement, especially in light of my frequent toing and froing up and down.

Then there are my fellow leaders, many of whom I have got to know quite well over the last few years. Some of them I know only by passing them during the day, but others I have enjoyed working alongside when jointly in charge of larger groups.

During the early summer of 2018, Scotland enjoyed a heatwave. Yes, you did read that correctly. There was no rain for several weeks and this creates a few problems in a country not known for its droughts. Leading groups in the mountains during that period presented a whole new set of challenges. Normally, I am looking out for clients by checking they are not getting too cold, or too wet, or offering them a dry pair of gloves, or finding a lunch spot sheltered from the worst of the gale. Not during the heatwave though, when the biggest hazards where suddenly sunburn, dehydration and heat stroke.

Then there was the issue of food. Living in the Cairngorms National Park, towards the east of the Highlands, quite often I will stay over on the west coast overnight if I have two or three consecutive days' work over there. Outdoor work is not particularly well paid, so anything you can do to save a few pounds in expenses is a good idea. One of my money-saving schemes is to take sandwiches across from home for all three days. This works fine most of the time, given average temperatures in Scotland mean that the boot of my car can act as a fridge. Lovely! Filling-wise, it doesn't really matter what you go for, although by the third day you obviously don't want the sandwich filling to be walking around by itself. Marmite would work fine in this regard, but Ellen sadly falls into the "hate it" part of the "You Either Love It Or Hate It" slogan. Inconvenient, but a small price to pay for an adoring wife.

During the 2018 heatwave, even I drew the line at keeping chicken or ham sandwiches in the boot of my car for three days. With temperatures regularly above 20 °C, that would not have ended well. Cheese, however, continued to work admirably. On the first day over there, I started with a cheese sandwich at the bottom of the hill. Three hours later at 25 °C and I had a cheese toasty. Genius! The sandwiches for the second and third days, residing quietly in the boot of my car, went through something analogous to the freeze-thaw process within the snowpack, so known amongst winter mountaineers. By the third day, the cheese would certainly be more akin to the cheese equivalent of *névé*, yet still perfectly palatable at the top of the Ben.

So impressed was I by the robustness and versatility of cheese as a sandwich filler, that rarely do I take any other sandwich filling on the hill these days. Of course, my esteemed outdoor colleagues quickly latched on to my worrying cheese habit, and so my nickname was coined - "the great big mouse of Ben Nevis".

As is probably apparent, I spend a fair bit of time on Ben Nevis. One of the most special times for me was in June 2019, when I had the privilege of accompanying Chris Clark on his own charity hike up Ben Nevis. Celebrating his 70th birthday year, Chris was raising money for Cancer Research UK, and had also generously pledged to match the amount of money raised to make an additional donation to Oakhaven Hospice, in Lymington. Chris did a fine job, cruising to the top in a shade over three hours.

Chris is truly an inspirational man, not only having come back from life-threatening illness and injury, but for his incredible contribution to the world of angling. Chris was very influential and inspiring to me during my time as a young member of the Lymington and District Sea Fishing Club during the 1990s. A former world shore angling champion and recognised as one of the world's best sea anglers, Chris has won an incredible number of world medals for individual, team and management performances. More recently, Chris has had a lead role in developing and coaching on the Angling Trust Talent Pathway, a training programme designed to help junior anglers transform into world-class anglers. Fittingly, Chris was recently awarded the British Citizen Award for Service to Education (BCAe) in recognition of his dedication to coaching young talent.

I was also delighted that Ellen agreed to pop over to Fort William in the evening. Chris and his wife very kindly treated us to a meal, and it was truly lovely to share time together. Ellen had heard plenty about this incredible man who could seemingly catch fish from an empty bucket! We were also privileged to see his BCAe. It was a pleasure and a privilege being on the hill with him that day, just as it was to fish alongside him all those years ago.

Chapter 19

Modern Times

The outdoor industry is very broad, so what is it I actually do? Primarily I have three work streams.

From the outset, it was my ambition to set up my own small business. After my first couple of years working for other outdoor activity providers, I took the plunge, and in 2019 set up my website for *James Orpwood Mountaineering*, offering year-round guided hill walking and mountain skills training. Needless to say, this was a daunting prospect. Providing content and photos to a website developer took a huge amount of work and that was just the beginning! As well as the financial investment in the website, I also bought good quality hire kit for my prospective clients. Costs of procuring crampons, ice axes, helmets, maps, map cases, compasses and ski goggles soon mount up, especially when everything is multiplied by six, my maximum group size. I also needed to produce standard operating procedures including risk assessments, incident report forms, route plan and late-back procedures, kit lists, participation forms etc. Coming up with promotional ideas was also a new challenge for me, although thankfully with a couple of years of freelancing behind me at that point, I had become pretty nifty with social media and I was well in the swing of things when it came to issuing invoices, recording expenses and suchlike. Additionally, I already had my insurance, First Aid qualification and memberships of professional bodies sorted for my freelance work, so that was a few other things taken care of.

Then there were lots of decisions to make. Did I want to offer "off the shelf" days which individuals could book as part of a larger group on pre-determined dates, or did I want to offer bespoke bookings for individuals and small groups on dates to suit them? Would anyone find my website? More importantly, would anyone want to book my services? How was I going to market myself? Where should I advertise?

It was a proud day when I took out my first client. In fact, it was a very proud day! With the support of Ellen, that day's work had come about entirely as a result of our own efforts. What an amazing feeling! Thankfully, several clients have followed and I am very proud to have had several clients through the door in my first year. Now well into my second year with this, it is just starting to pick up well and I am excited about developing my own small business into the future.

My other two work streams are true to how I started. I work on a freelance basis for a number of outdoor activity providers, leading mountain activities such as guided walks (summer and winter), charity and challenge events, navigation and winter skills courses. This sort of work is very rewarding and generally pretty good fun - about as close to "getting paid to go hill walking" as you can probably get. The instructional aspects associated with running a navigation course or a winter skills course are particularly rewarding.

Finally, I work for an adventure travel company. Still as a freelancer, this involves guiding groups on an adventure travel holiday, based around a theme such as walking, or a multi-activity basis when other activities such as mountain biking might also take place. I find it interesting to note how other people perceive this work. For example, through the summer I will often get asked, rather sarcastically, "Oh, are you on holiday again next week?" I will usually laugh this off politely, but will think to myself, "No, I am not. The clients are on holiday; I shall be working incredibly hard to give them the best experience I possibly can."

Here is a brief snapshot of what such work might entail for a typical trip.

I shall be researching walking routes and logistics up to a year before the clients' holiday is due to start. I shall be finding out where the hotels and other attractions in their itinerary are, if I am not already familiar with them. I shall spend the long, dark winter evenings researching aspects of Scottish history/food/culture/mythology/you name it, to share with the clients, hoping to enrich their experience and tap in to their individual interests. I shall spend the day before the trip packing all my kit and making final preparations, ringing around various hotels, restaurants and other activity providers to double-check reservations and suchlike, and making sure I am up to speed with any special dietary requirements or medical conditions clients may have. I am always thinking ahead for how to maximise the clients' experience, often without realising it! Once on the trip, I will be getting paid. Why shouldn't I? I am a highly-qualified and experienced professional, after all. I am a Winter ML, a tour guide, a driver, a host, a photographer, a diplomat, a translator, a liaison officer, a first aider, an entertainer, a cleaner, a catering assistant, a logistics coordinator and a budget holder, among other things (historian, geologist, psychologist, current affairs commentator, to name a few).

A typical day might pan out as follows. I shall be up by 6 a.m. to sort myself out, check the route for the day (again!), check the weather forecast (again!), brush the van out and collect the packed lunches. It goes without saying that clients' experience during activity days must go without a hitch, so I must be very familiar with the route so I can fully concentrate on ensuring the clients have a great day. Mary and Jim are at the back a lot. Are they just a bit slower than everyone else, or do they not like the rest of the group? Sandra is travelling by herself. I need to make an extra effort to make sure she doesn't feel left out of the group. Dave is hard of hearing. I'll need to remember that and make sure he can see my mouth when I'm speaking. Oh, and it's Claire's birthday tomorrow. I must remember to slip off for a few minutes when we get back to the hotel and buy her a wee cake. Ah, she's allergic to dairy, so I'll see what the hotel can help with to sort a little birthday treat for her. We'll be able to see that famous castle soon so I need to gather the group together by then so I can explain a bit about its history. OK, it seems this group isn't particularly into its history, but they're a bunch of medics and geologists, so maybe I'll point out some interesting geology to them later, and explain why the cliffs we're coming to are effectively "upside down".

Back at the hotel and I may get a chance to take a breath when the guests have unloaded and headed off for showers. It's a chance to have a shower myself and work on a plan for tomorrow so I can brief the guests at dinner. But first that wee job with Tom's walking poles - where did I put my screwdriver?

At dinner I must be a perfect host. (This can be far harder than leading any walk or bike ride!) Does this group want me to tell them jokes (hopefully not, for their sake), explain how the Scottish Wars of Independence came about, or ask them what their children are studying at university?

If it's a big group they almost certainly don't all want the same thing. Jack is in his 70s, and is quite a character, often telling me his tales of exploits with the ladies earlier in life. But Claire and Tom appear to be quite serious and deeply religious. I don't want them to be offended by Jack's stories, and anyway, they seem much more interested in my early life as a research scientist. Meanwhile, Sandra really seems to appreciate the extra effort I have made to make her feel part of the group, but has clearly had a bit too much wine with dinner. I wish I'd remembered to wear my wedding ring today.

I won't leave dinner until the last client has retired for the evening - that would seem rude, so after 10 p.m. I finally leave to head back to my accommodation a short drive away. Should I re-pack my rucksack tonight? No, the kit is still drying out from today and, anyway, it will be quicker in the morning. It's been a 16-hour day and I haven't stopped. I'll just get up a bit earlier and do it first thing …

So no, it's not a holiday; it's work but I just happen to love it. There is an enormous sense of satisfaction when a client hands you a card at the end of a trip and it states their trip has exceeded all expectations. And that's the key. If they use the phrase "my trip" or "our trip", you've done something right as they feel as if it was their holiday, made for them, even though they were possibly part of a larger group. Now it's time to return to base, clean the van, sort the kit, write a trip report and tally all the finances. That'll be tomorrow's job. Then there's time to reflect. What went well? What didn't go so well? Did the walking routes work for this group? Where else could we look at going next time? I didn't know that other castle was there - I must find out a bit about that.

One of the most significant things I was told many years ago, was that to work successfully in the outdoors, simply loving the outdoors is not enough. Of course you must love the outdoors. That goes without saying. But you must also love sharing it with people. I wouldn't make a very good host on an adventure travel holiday if I didn't love sharing experiences with people! Reflecting back to my quieter younger self, living a very solitary life, I wonder, how would he see what I do now, and what I have achieved? Like our group's leader in Bolivia, does all the preparation I put in to a trip make it look seemingly effortless to the clients? Like the many leaders, guides and instructors I know, do I have that calm yet inspiring presence and that encouraging confidence, to set my clients' minds at ease? Do I have the engaging manner, and the sparkle of fun which comes from being somewhere I love, doing something I love? I hope so. It is great, both personally and in terms of future business, to see warm reviews from clients, especially when particular reference is made to my qualities (as they see them!) or to a specific thing that I went out of my way to do for them.

I mentioned earlier how incredibly diverse the outdoor industry is. A common theme among the most successful of practitioners is their infectious love of what they do and how they pass that on, be that teaching hard skills, explaining a little about mountain flora and fauna, coaching a nervous child to reach their personal high point on a climbing wall, or simply enjoying the thrill which goes with making something special happen for a client. For me, these are the key things. Firstly, I love introducing people to the environment which I love so much, and one which gives me so much joy and pleasure. Secondly, I love enabling people to do things which maybe they wouldn't be able to do if I wasn't there. This might be taking somebody up Ben Nevis in winter if they're not too confident of their ability to navigate the summit plateau successfully in a whiteout. It might be teaching someone how to take a compass bearing and how to interpret contour lines on a map, increasing their confidence to explore the mountains independently. It might be showing them how to use crampons and an ice axe, helping them with their transition to winter hill walking. One of the many great things about the outdoors in its widest context is that regardless of your current skill level and experience, there will always be something available to challenge you. This notion that all individuals have a personal goal, and that in my work I can help people to achieve their goal, is immensely satisfying, regardless of what the goal might be.

The master plan is that by having three strands to my income, if any one of them starts to dry up, I can hopefully make up for it by pushing the other two. Of course, it would be lovely to increase the emphasis on my own small business, but all in good time. During these early years, I have enjoyed the variety in my work, and am getting to the stage where, to a greater or lesser extent, I can pick and choose what work I do and who I work for.

I love what I do, and how many of us can truly say that of our work?

Chapter 20

Reflections

Clearly, many things have changed since I first came to Scotland 18 years ago. Whilst out and about with clients, I am not always chatting or following a compass bearing or stuffing my face with food, contrary to popular belief. Often clients will be content to meander at their own pace, enjoying their surroundings and just being there, perhaps with family or friends. This gives me moments to reflect and on many occasions I have looked around where I am and thought, "Wow, I can't believe I'm being paid to do this." Indeed, there are some clients who prove to be so affable that it is just like having a day out with a friend.

Even prior to working in the outdoors, I have always believed the mountains are a great leveller. When you're up in the mountains, the normal stuff in life becomes irrelevant. Looking after yourself in the mountains is not affected by how much money you have in the bank, what job you have, how many degrees you have, etc. This has been demonstrated to me time and time again. For example, I have had the pleasure of working with a number of corporate groups who have opted to do a team-building day by walking up and down Ben Nevis. As should always be the case, my fellow leaders and I treat every client as an individual. We have no idea, until or unless it comes up in conversation, what role in their organisation any of the clients have, be they the CEO or the cleaner. We are there to work as a team to try and complete an objective. Mountains do not respect titles, roles, bank balances or any other human constraints. Indeed, the same is pretty much true of any clients. At the start of a day or week, all I have is a list of clients' names. I may have spoken with them on the phone or exchanged a few emails, and will know a little about their prior experience, medical history and the like. However, information regarding job title, salary and bank balance is not discussed. For what I do and love, these things are irrelevant and all the better for it.

During the course of my time with clients, at some point the conversation often drifts along the lines of, "How does a fisheries scientist end up working in the outdoors?" This may be preceded with a polite (or not so polite) hint as to the fact my accent suggests very strongly that perhaps I am not originally from Scotland. If and when my previous career crops up in conversation with clients, many will express a degree of surprise. I'm not sure if I should be offended by this - perhaps I just don't look all that clever?! It is always fun to laugh this off and, given the wonders of modern technology and internet search engines, clients frequently know more about my previous career than I do. More often than not, clients are genuinely intrigued by my apparently drastic career change, and if this crops up early on, it is a good ice breaker as it can inject a bit of good humour into proceedings.

Any questions about whether my new career offers me sufficient mental stimulation, and the answer is very definitely, yes! No doubt, however, my chosen profession is underrated by others, particularly those who think I should get a "proper job". The activities themselves can be incredibly absorbing, for example, leading clients safely to Ben Macdui and back in a whiteout certainly sharpens the mind when it comes to navigation, and that's before you've considered anything else. Each day brings a new and unique set of challenges and considerations, even when working somewhere I may have been many times before. At the very least, the clients are different, so the needs of those clients will not be the same as last time I was there. Even if their needs are similar, the weather (which will also have changed) will dictate how I respond to those needs. Winter skills courses are a prime example of this. Clearly, any plan for a two-day winter skills course will have to be tailored to what is possible and safe at the time. The weather and avalanche forecasts and the prevailing conditions of the snowpack will dictate where we go and what we do. Flexibility and adaptability are key, and trying to work out plans A, B and C (and often it'll be plan D which ends up happening) keeps me on my toes and is very absorbing.

Then there are the many issues surrounding group management skills. As with any skill set, the finer points of group management techniques and strategies can only really be developed, refined and honed with increased exposure to "real-world" clients, figuring out what works and what doesn't work in various situations. No course can really prepare you for this, I think, and it's where experience really plays a huge part. In fact, I truly believe you could lead in the mountains for longer than any lifetime and still learn something every time you go out. In this regard, as well as the obvious skills of clear verbal communication, "reading" your clients, their facial expressions and their body language, thinking ahead, and trying to pre-empt what is likely to happen, can be hugely beneficial. Clients will typically copy what you *do* and not necessarily absorb what you *say*, so something as simple as stopping for a drink can encourage your clients to do likewise. The makeup of a group can also be very revealing. For example, if I am leading a group of six lads in their 20s, and I stop half way up a hill and ask if anybody is getting cold, the chances of any of them admitting to being cold is next to zero! However, if I say, "You know what lads, I'm getting a bit cold, I'm just going to stop and put on an extra layer and a hat", I will probably find that at least some of them will copy me, albeit with a few mumbles of, "I'm not really cold but I might as well." Perhaps the fact my brain gets used to such an extent now is subconsciously one of the reasons I love what I do so much?

I am a firm believer that no experience in life is ever wasted. I know of several people working in the outdoors who initially trained and qualified to do something very different. The key thing is to recognise whether you would rather be doing something else, and doing something positive about it if that is the case. "Transferable skills" is something of a catchphrase in relation to seeking employment in general, and my early scientific career certainly gave me plenty of those. The development of good writing skills is a key skill in science, and I shall leave it up to you to decide whether mine are any good! Current project aside, I do enjoy writing occasional articles for outdoor magazines. Similarly with presentation skills - a key scientific skill, yet one which has served me well when presenting photos and tales from my travels and mountain adventures on several occasions. Looking back even further, the time I spent working in customer-facing roles in a supermarket remains some of my most valuable work experience to date. This is particularly relevant now as I run my own small business and work with clients in a customer-facing and customer-focussed role.

I am also a firm believer that in life you cannot have everything. There are always choices to be made, and inevitably some sacrifices need to be made in order to follow a particular path. For Ellen and I, one of the big sacrifices is living a relatively long way from the rest of our respective families. We therefore make every effort to maximise the quality of the limited time we spend with our families.

In this regard, the Lake District is still an important part of my life. I love it very much, but it is not fair to compare it to the Highlands of Scotland. They are very different places, and I love spending time in each of them. Indeed, I would like to spend more time working and playing in the Lake District, but it can be difficult to justify the five hours of driving from home, considering the other options available much closer by. Helpfully, much as my parents enjoy occasional forays to Scotland, over the years we have used the Lake District as a convenient half-way point to spend a few days together. This is a great privilege as many people I know simply do not have the option to spend time with their parents anymore. They also understand that, being self-employed, it is difficult to turn down work opportunities. Yet it is really important to do just that occasionally, defending time for myself to spend with family and friends, or to gain further experience towards future qualifications. Inevitably, there will come a time when I am no longer able to spend time with my parents, and I do not want to be counted among those people who wish they had spent more time with their loved ones.

Thankfully, just like that walk up to Loch Etchachan with my parents in 2006, I cast my mind back many years to when I was just ten years old, and the occasion when we were "temporarily cartographically challenged" on the fells above Watendlath. As an outdoor professional, it would be great to say nothing similar has ever happened in recent times, but that would not be telling the truth, would it?! Fair to say my parents, Ellen and I have shared a fair few epics in recent years whilst enjoying holidays together in the Lake District.

On one occasion, we had taken the launch across Derwent Water and had been on a long walk. I don't recall exactly where, but the long and short of it was we ended up on the top of Cat Bells late in the day. Cat Bells is well loved, having been many people's first "mountain" they climbed. The views from the top adorn many a chocolate box, and it is a lovely spot. Usually very busy, on this particular afternoon it was suspiciously quiet. Descending back to Kitchen Bay, and the launch which would take us effortlessly back across to our accommodation in Keswick, the reality suddenly dawned on us as to why it was so quiet. The last launch of the day had been and gone some time ago! After drinking the last of our coffee and eating a few Jaffa cakes, we had no option but to walk the extra three miles back to Keswick via Portinscale. Normally this is a pleasant stroll, but not after the long day we had done.

A similar thing happened one September day when we had headed out for a substantial walk in Borrowdale. Making the most of the excellent local buses meant we could start and finish in different places. Starting in Seatoller, we walked through to Seathwaite before climbing up past Stockley Bridge beside Grains Gill. We then followed the high-level route through to Angle Tarn before descending from Stake Pass to walk the length of Langstrath back to Stonethwaite, then Rosthwaite, planning to catch the bus back to our accommodation from there. However, being September, it dawned on us somewhere around Stake Pass that it would soon be dark. With a renewed sense of urgency, we made a swift descent along Langstrath, ending up back in Rosthwaite. Despite rushing to beat the onset of darkness, we had missed the last bus, but we did have coffee and Jaffa cakes. A definite theme is emerging here! We then "enjoyed" an additional seven-mile walk back to Keswick, in the dark, with our headlamps picking out occasional pairs of eyes in the deserted darkness. It never occurred to any of us to call a taxi.

It is such epics which we remember and still talk about.

So, what about the future? I hope it is obvious that I love what I do, and I intend to carry on running my own small business alongside my freelance work and my adventure travel work for a long time to come. But that doesn't mean the dream stops here. There are several things I still want to achieve.

I would love to think that, with sufficient time and dedication, I can progress to the higher qualifications in mountaineering, namely the Mountaineering and Climbing Instructor (MCI) qualification, followed by its winter counterpart. These qualifications open up the world of teaching and leading all aspects of mountaineering and climbing in the UK and Ireland. This will once again require a focussed and determined commitment. Over the last 18 years, I have developed a great wealth of year-round hill walking and general mountaineering experience and judgement. I can lead climbs graded Severe on rock. In winter, I lead up to Scottish grade II and I am happy to climb grade III or even grade IV when someone else is on the sharp end of the rope. Clearly there is a long journey ahead if I am going to succeed in this regard. However, I am reminded of the famous quote by the late Alex Lowe, a famous American mountaineer; "The best climber is the one having the most fun."

REFLECTIONS

It would be great to expand my own small business to shift the emphasis of my work increasingly towards my own clients and services. There are also several places around the world where I would like to climb, most notably Peru. I would also like to "complete" the Munros at some point. I have climbed almost half of Scotland's mountains over 3,000 ft, but working professionally in the outdoors creates a topsy-turvy world when I have been up some of the Munros many, many times - Ben Nevis, Stob Ban (Mamores), Ben Macdui, Cairn Gorm, Sgor Gaoith, Bynack More, to name a few of my regulars with clients - and of course my personal favourites, Cairn Toul and Braeriach. It would also be fantastic to do lots more climbing, which will help with some of the above, and continue to carry out thorough reconnaissance trips for my adventure travel work.

Yet most of all, I hope I can keep myself fit and healthy enough to enjoy Scotland and all it has to offer for as long as possible. I hope Ellen is around for a long time yet to share these future aspirations, having been so influential in achieving our dream together. Our trip to Nepal in 2008 changed both our lives beyond all recognition and hopefully it is obvious, for the better! Starting that adventure took just one phone call.

Choosing to pursue a drastically different career path from the one for which I originally trained was not easy. There were many doubts and fears along the way, not least of all leaving a steady job with a reliable income and turning my hobby and passion into my career once again. But, I reasoned, surely it is better to try, and risk failure, than not to try at all? Sadly, plenty of people do live to regret things they haven't done - yet all they had to do was decide to make it happen, or at least try. On that basis, I decided to pursue my dream - my own quest for professional and personal fulfilment in the mountains. I hope the story of my journey inspires you.

"All men dream: but not equally. Those who dream by night in the dusty recesses of their minds wake in the day to find that it was vanity: but the dreamers of the day are dangerous men, for they may act their dreams with open eyes, to make it possible."

T. E. Lawrence, *Seven Pillars of Wisdom*

Epilogue

I was alone on top of Stob Coire an t-Sneachda, eating my lunch and gazing at the mountains all around. It was a beautiful day in mid-March 2020 and, unusually for the Cairngorms, there was not a breath of wind. The plateau stretched away behind me towards Ben Macdui. The shapely form of Cairn Toul, one of my favourite mountains, made its presence felt on the far side of the Lairig Ghru. Close by the slopes of Cairn Gorm resembled pâté, the strengthening power of the sun at this time of year creating a mottled patchwork of snow and rocks. Spring had already arrived on the lower hills on the far side of Glenmore, with the greens of the forest and the browns of the heather-covered slopes framing the deep blue waters of Loch Morlich. I loved it here. I felt so at home. I had been here so many times before, to this exact spot. In fact, I had been here earlier that day. Sadly, I had no idea when I would next be able to visit here, or indeed any mountain.

Earlier in the day I had wandered up in to Coire an t-Sneachda. Ellen was in work and, given how quiet it was, it seemed the rest of humanity was too. I had enjoyed the rare feeling of sun on my face and wished I had my sunglasses with me. From the flat area in the back of the corrie I had studied the great cliffs carefully, intending to solo one of the easy gullies. Conditions were excellent as the recent period of freeze-thaw cycles had left the gullies full of beautifully consolidated hard snow. I eventually settled on Central Gully (grade I), a route I had climbed several years previously whilst preparing for my Winter ML assessment. I geared up, crossed the boulder field, headed up the increasingly steep snow to the bottom of the route and into the gully itself. As expected, it was in excellent condition. My crampons bit reassuringly into the snow and my ice axe placements felt secure and positive. It was so good that when I topped out, I walked around the rim of the corrie via the top of Stob Coire an t-Sneachda and proceeded to Windy Col. From there, I dropped back into the corrie below the Mess of Pottage and traversed on steep snow to the foot of Aladdin's Couloir (grade I). This second climb of the day offered similarly good conditions and soon I was on top of Stob Coire an t-Sneachda for the second time that day.

As I sat there in the sun it was so peaceful, difficult to imagine how terribly COVID-19 was affecting life in Europe. Declared the active centre of the worldwide pandemic by the World Health Organisation (WHO), extensive lockdown measures were already in place across mainland Europe and I was fully expecting similar measures to be applied in the UK very soon. (An enforced lockdown would be announced in the UK just days later.) With this in mind, many outdoor professionals, myself included, had already cancelled their work for the foreseeable future. We did not want to encourage folk to travel to the Highlands, for fear of spreading the virus and putting extra pressure on the relatively limited NHS resources in our rural communities. I knew that, in all likelihood, my summer season's work programme with other providers would also be reduced to nothing because of the COVID-19 outbreak and related restrictions on movement. I knew the devastating impact COVID-19 would have not only on my business, but many thousands of businesses up and down the country, and indeed around the world, in all sorts of industries.

From the top of Stob Coire an t-Sneachda I thought of Ellen. It wasn't too difficult. Far below, I could just about make out the stream which runs in to Loch Morlich, where I had proposed to Ellen over a decade previously. Almost everywhere I looked brought back a memory of a special time together. I thought back over the years of effort Ellen and I had put in to get us where we were today. Ellen and I have been told many times that we are lucky to live where we do, and it has often been said I am lucky to be doing something I love. Yet, these things did not come about as the result of some chance "lucky" event. Working together, Ellen and I decided to do what we've done and it took many years of hard work, dedication and commitment to make it happen. Those telling us may have forgotten, or simply be unaware of, the sacrifices we made along the way. It was not easy to live apart for all those years as a married couple, but we did this to make our transition to a different way of life more secure financially. Then there are the practical considerations of how I earn my money - no guaranteed income, no job security, no regular pay cheque each month, no paid holidays, no sick pay, no employer's pension scheme etc. By the same token, this is not "bad luck" but choices made freely, fully accepting their implications because of the amazing quality of life we enjoy. That day, facing the prospect of losing an entire season's work in the blink of an eye, it was heart-wrenching to think all our efforts might be about to prove futile.

I quickly reminded myself that, far worse than any economic impact, a human tragedy similar to the one being experienced in mainland Europe was expected in the UK, with many thousands of deaths predicted in the coming weeks. Tragically, I knew that each and every victim - a loved mother, father, sister, brother, son, daughter, grandmother, grandfather, niece, nephew, cousin, friend or colleague - was a person who undoubtedly touched many lives in a positive way. Suddenly, the minor inconvenience of not being able to climb a mountain seemed slightly trivial, despite the fact my livelihood now depended upon it.

It was a strange feeling, not knowing when I would next be back in the mountains, but I knew it would not be for quite some time. I got up and started walking, slowly for once, in the general direction of the car park. I didn't want to leave. The sun was warming the back of my head. My crampons bit pleasingly into the hard snow. A small group of reindeer grazed peacefully near the top of Coire Raibeirt. All looked well with the world up here that day, and it was just *so* beautiful. I hoped I would be able to return soon, perhaps at night next winter. I knew that in the darkness of a clear Cairngorms' winter night, I would be able to look up and see Orion's Belt - those three beautiful stars which connect my past with the present and, God willing, my future with Ellen. Before beginning my descent from the plateau, I turned and looked back. I could see Loch Etchachan nestling in its little Arctic hollow, just as it always did. It was beautiful. I had no regrets.

Acknowledgements

Many people have assisted with the production of this book.

I would like to thank Roger Bayzand for kindly agreeing to write the Foreword, and Pauline Sanderson and Chris Clark for their warm reviews. Each of you has had a special part to play in the journey described in this book, so thank you for the inspiration and great memories too.

I am also grateful to the many people who readily allowed their photographs to be included in this book.

I would also like to thank Fiona, my eldest sister, and her husband, for painstakingly reviewing and proof-reading successive drafts of the manuscript, and for gener-ous financial support with production costs. Thank you for your continual encouragement, even responding enthusias-tically when the 20th version of the cover appeared in your inboxes!

Of course, I must thank my family for always being there for me, for their love, and for introducing me to the delights of both the aquatic world and the mountains at a young age.

Finally, I must thank my wonderful wife, Ellen, not only for our mutual love, care and devotion to each other, but for her being so instrumental in enabling us to achieve our dream, together.

James Orpwood
July 2020

Selected Bibliography And Further Reading

First-Time Latin America. Polly Rodger Brown & James Read (2006). 2nd Edition. Rough Guides, London.

View From The Summit. Sir Edmund Hillary (2000). Corgi Books, Transworld Publishers, London.

The Munros: Scotland's Highest Mountains. Cameron McNeish (1996). Lomond Books, Edinburgh.

Trekking And Climbing The Andes. Val Pitkethly & Kate Harper (2008). 2nd Edition. New Holland Publishers (UK) Ltd., London.

Trekking And Climbing In Nepal. Steve Razzetti (2000). Globetrotter Adventure Guide. New Holland Publishers (UK) Ltd., London.

The World's Longest Climb. Pauline Sanderson (2011). Grafika Ltd., Derbyshire, UK.

The Living Mountain. Nan Shepherd (2011). Canongate Books, Edinburgh.

Trekking In The Atlas Mountains. Karl Smith (2004). 3rd Edition. Cicerone Press, Cumbria, UK.

About The Author

James has a passion for sharing his love of Scotland's mountains and wild places with others. From his home in the Cairngorms National Park where he lives with his wife, Ellen, James runs his own small business, *James Orpwood Mountaineering*, offering year-round guided hill walking and mountain skills training. James also works as a freelance outdoor instructor for other outdoor activity providers.

A qualified Winter Mountain Leader, Summer Mountain Leader, Rock Climbing Instructor, Climbing Wall Instructor and Trail Cycle Leader, James also holds the National Navigation Award Scheme (NNAS) Tutor Award. James also has a First Class Honours Degree and a PhD from his days as a fisheries scientist.

Website: www.jamesorpwoodmountaineering.co.uk
Facebook: @JamesOrpwoodMountaineering

Above left: The author enjoying a coffee in the mountains. © Ellen Thornell, 2010. **Above right:** Logo designed by Coire Creative, Aviemore. © *James Orpwood Mountaineering*, 2020.

Lightning Source UK Ltd.
Milton Keynes UK
UKHW051117141120
373352UK00008B/266

9 781839 752438